New Studies in the Philosophy of Religion

General Editor: W. D. Hudson, Reader in Moral Philosophy,
University of Exeter

This series of monographs includes studies of all the main problems in the philosophy of religion. It will be of particular interest to those who study this subject in universities or colleges. The philosophical problems connected with religious belief are not, however, a subject of concern only to specialists; they arise in one form or another for all intelligent men when confronted by the appeals or the claims of religion.

The general approach of this series is from the standpoint of contemporary analytical philosophy, and the monographs are written by a distinguished team of philosophers, all of whom now teach, or have recently taught, in British or American universities. Each author has been commissioned to analyse some aspect of religious belief; to set forth clearly and concisely the philosophical problems which arise from it; to take into account the solutions which classical or contemporary philosophers have offered; and to present his own critical assessment of how religious belief now stands in the light of these problems and their proposed solutions.

In the main it is theism with which these monographs deal, because that is the type of religious belief with which readers are most likely to be familiar, but other forms of religion are not ignored. Some of the authors are religious believers and some are not, but it is not their primary aim to write polemically, much less dogmatically, for or against religion. Rather, they set themselves to clarify the nature of religious belief in the light of modern philosophy by bringing into focus the questions about it which a reasonable man as such has to ask. How is talk of God like, and how unlike, other universes of discourse in which men engage, such as science, art or morality? Is this talk of God self-consistent? Does it accord with other rational beliefs which we hold about man or the world which he inhabits? It is questions such as these which this series will help the reader to answer for himself.

New Studies in the Philosophy of Religion

IN THE SAME SERIES

Published

Jonathan Barnes *The Ontological Argument*
W. W. Bartley III *Morality and Religion*
Michael Durrant *The Logical Status of 'God'*
Thomas McPherson *The Argument from Design*
T. R. Miles *Religious Experience*
Kai Nielsen *Scepticism*
Humphrey Palmer *Analogy*
D. Z. Phillips *Death and Immortality*
Vernon Pratt *Religion and Secularisation*
Ninian Smart *The Concept of Worship*
Richard Swinburne *The Concept of Miracle*

In preparation

W. D. Hudson *Wittgenstein's Influence on the Philosophy of Religion*
David Jenkins *The Authenticity of Faith: Existentialist Theology
    and the Problem of the Knowledge of God*
D. J. O'Connor *The Cosmological Argument*
I. T. Ramsey *The Problem of Evil*

Analogy

A Study of Qualification and Argument in Theology

HUMPHREY PALMER

Senior Lecturer in Philosophy, University College, Cardiff

Macmillan

First published 1973 by
THE MACMILLAN PRESS LTD
London and Basingstoke
Associated companies in New York Dublin
Melbourne Johannesburg and Madras

SBN 333 10494 3

Photoset and printed by
REDWOOD PRESS LIMITED
Trowbridge, Wiltshire

to
பாக்கியம்
and
மோஹன்

Contents

General Editor's Preface   xi

Author's Preface   xiii

A Letter   xv

1. Do We Need a Theory of Analogy?

    I IS SOME NONSENSE RELIGIOUS?   3
       Are religious statements intelligible (6) only
       to believers, or (7) to those with a 'higher'
       knowledge, or (9) do they all need interpreting?
       (12) This book an inquiry, not an apology.

    II DANGER: PARLIAMENT AT WORK   7
       The 'wisdom' of Parliament, (9) taken in a
       special sense, (12) to humbug us. (17) Reli-
       gious parallels, taken as (18) plain humbug,
       (19) venial muddle.

    III ANALOGY AND ARGUMENTS   15
       Theory of Analogy (5) spoils arguments. (8)
       Borrowing of terms common. (11) Our discus-
       sion limited to Christianity. (12) Difference
       between analysis and interpretation. (13) Sim-
       plist objection answered.

2. The Theory in Outline

    IV MEANING WHAT WE SAY   25
       Religious terms bear a qualified sense, (4)
       necessarily, say some, as God is infinite. (11)
       The Postulate of Univocity and the growth of
       words. (16) Humpty Dumpty. (18) Definition
       keeps meaning public. (23) Private meaning
       impractical.

V SAYING WHAT WE MEAN
Analogy as semi-ambiguity, (7) stated in equation form (13) with two unknowns, (15) useless for calculation but (18) indicates a formal relationship.

3. Some Details of the Theory

VI WHAT ELEPHANTS AREN'T   47
Denials can be taken literally, but (7) will not tell us anything. (17) Few preach ineffability.

VII WHAT WE CAN'T SAY CLEARER   55
Symbols we cannot see behind, (3) used in faith that creatures must resemble God. (8) What the words really mean is right, only we can't make it out (!).

VIII IS THE THEORY SUBJECT TO ANALOGY?   61
Proof that there is a God wrongly thought exempt, to stop theory undermining itself. (8) The qualification 'known to be' may avoid this difficulty.

IX IRREDUCIBLES   67
Reducing symbols (8) to other symbols, (10) any of which may be subject to analogy.

X BEING TOLD THE RIGHT THING TO SAY   72
God as cause has all creation's perfections; (7) and the bad ones too? (14) Truths we fail to express can only be taken on trust. (17) Trust also needed for preferring some statements as failing better.

4. Effect of the Theory on Theology

XI NOT PROVEN   81
The theory is unprovable, and (6) disastrous for theology.

XII ARGUING BY METAPHOR   85
*Metaphor, simile, allegory. (8) Analogy
useful as suggesting arguments, (10) not in
place of them. (17) Explicit and implicit analogies (18) both need checking. (21) Uncheckable analogies help us to go on talking.*

XIII ANALOGY SPOILS ARGUMENTS   97
*Theology, unlike prayer, depends on argument,
which (6) analogy debilitates; (11) for not
even validity can be known with unintelligible
terms. (14) Views of Hume, (16) Maimonides, (17) Aquinas. (23) This flaw debunks
everyone's theology.* ·

5. Some Objections to the Theory
XIV CONTEXTUAL DETERMINATION OF MEANING   113
*Mistaken argument that a complete and work-
ing language-game cannot be a big mistake.
(14) Context determines meaning to varying
extents. (20) Interpretation or analysis. (25)
Technical terms fixed by definitions.*

XV FAMILY RESEMBLANCES   125
*Single-essence theory of definition (4) held in-
adequate to* games, knowledge, *etc. (6)
Cross-classification. (9) Stretching a point.
(14) Family view applies to distinct senses of
some words but (15) not to any terms.*

XVI BORROWING   131
*In science, loan-words redeemed by observation
and theory. (7) Irredeemables useful for speculation only. (10) Speculation is not science.*

6. Reforming Theology to Suit the Theory
XVII DOGMATIC SYSTEMS   139
*Theology, if deductive and descriptive, destroy-
ed by analogy.*

XVIII FIVE WAYS NOWHERE   143
    Literalism, (2) Nonsensicalism, (3) Fideism,
    (7) Fundamentalism (16) Mysticalism.

XIX NONDESCRIPTIVISM   152
    Not right because others wrong. (5) Affirma-
    tions and assertions. (11) Conflict of vows.
    (19) Life-challenges. (24) Revising vows.
    (27) Looking for challenges.

XX PROPER FAITH   161
    In religion, beliefs not primary. (4) How to
    choose a religious symbol-set. (9) Our impres-
    sion of Jesus as a man may incline us to take
    his theology on trust.

Appendix: Texts from Aquinas's discus-   165
sions of analogy

Notes   177

Index   185

References given in the Notes are signalled
in the text by *, comments and further
quotations by †.

General Editor's Preface

PHILOSOPHERS of religion have concerned themselves for a long time with logical problems arising from the use of analogy. Within many systems of belief the view has prevailed that God can only be spoken about analogically and philosophers have asked themselves both what precisely it means to hold this view and what follows concerning religious language once it is accepted.

In particular, there is the problem of the nature and extent of the price which has to be paid when language is used analogically. Is it so high a price that the things said of God become unintelligible; or is it simply that we cannot draw inferences from them in the way that we might if they were said of man? Dr. Palmer's view is that God can be talked about but not argued about. He supports it in this monograph by an original and interesting analysis which, though it deals with the profoundest matters, does so with a light and lucid touch. His book will interest professional philosophers, but will be found readable and thought-provoking by all who have an interest in religion.

W. D. HUDSON

University of Exeter

Author's Preface

I have cause to be grateful to many who have written on Analogy, and especially to those with whom I disagree. Quite a few of them are mentioned in the Notes. Not mentioned there are several kind friends who helped on this point or that; nor Mrs M. Rees, who typed a lot of it.

Some of the things said in this book have been said to groups in Bridgend, Cardiff, Lampeter, Cambridge, Exeter, Poona and Dharwar, from whom I received useful comments, and encouragement. Some parts have been published before, in other, and maybe clearer, terms: in 'Affirmation and Assertion', *Philosophy* (1964) 120f.; 'To Reduce and to Locate', *Listener* (1966) 605f, 647f.; 'Understanding First', *Theology* (1968) 107f.; and *The Logic of Gospel Criticism* (1968) 198f.

The views put forward here are, I gather, Arian, Pelagian, Symbolist, and almost Theothanatarian. Perhaps those who go by the label ought to consult a book containing safer thoughts. These are readily available.   HUMPHREY PALMER

Cardiff
September 1972.

A Letter, 1965, about a Broadcast Talk

Dear Sir,

It is difficult, says Professor X, to argue with the 'new theologians' because they won't say what they mean. For instance, they don't believe that Jesus rose from the dead, but they go on saying he did, *meaning* that Christians, since his death, have had a new sort of experience . . . but if that's what they mean, why not *say so*?

Professor X's wit and skill, in posing this question, may divert attention from the difficulty all theologians have in meaning what they say. For if all our terms derive from our earthly experience, how can any of them be applied to God? If theologians use words in their ordinary sense, their theology will be anthropomorphic. If on the other hand a term is to mean something quite different when applied to God, then theology is incomprehensible. With grateful thanks to St Thomas, Professor X takes the middle way, holding that the meaning of any term in theology, though different, is yet somehow related to its ordinary use. In his well-known book on the subject, he tried manfully to work out just what that relation is. Neither he nor his readers will suppose the answer to be easy or obvious. His easy and obvious satire on the 'new theology' therefore comes as a surprise.

The same problem faces both parties. Traditionalists do their theology first, as though it were an exact science, and worry about the interpretation afterwards. Liberals hold that the question of interpretation should be taken first: for if none of the things said about God can be understood quite literally, their metaphorical meanings must be allowed for in the doing of theology. The current proposal is (I think) to give up inference ('God is holy *therefore...*') and to restrict preaching to doctrines which come home to us directly in our moral and social experience. A creed, they say, must be able to be lived out, if it is to be commended to others for belief.

The 'new theology' is not of course new. It is not, strictly speaking, theology, but an essay in metatheology; a discussion of how we can know what we mean when we say things about God. That discussion is difficult, and sometimes technical. Hence the temptation, in a popular presentation, to state an opponent's position in a form which, while not expressing his intentions, fits in with some of his statements, is easy to explain, and good fun to ridicule.

It is time both sides stopped playing to the gallery. There is work to be done.

Yours faithfully
H.P.

1. Do We Need a Theory of Analogy?

1 Is Some Nonsense Religious?

PEOPLE do say odd things about God, and about The Universe.

2 Should we take them to mean precisely what they say? Can we even expect to understand? Or is that only granted to initiates?

3 Are we – the public – intended to believe, to accept as true, what these people say? Because *they* say it, or because of the reasons they offer in support?

4 If for reasons, are these people open to counter-argument? Will they accept ordinary, well-tried, proper, objective standards for deciding whether their arguments are sound? Or must they always appeal to some special and favourable 'higher' court?

5 The prophets and mystics and philosophers who first made these remarkable statements did not have to face an interrogation of this sort. But it has to be faced by disciples who commend their words to the world at large. In their replies we can make out three distinct lines of defence.

6 Some say that such statements will only be understood by those 'inside'. Only those who believe in an Absolute will ask how it is related to the process of our seemingly changing world. None except Christians need say, or can follow, the creed called Athanasian.

7 Others – not liking to suggest that religion is

some sort of club – speak of two 'levels' of knowledge. There is everyday knowledge, based on ordinary experience, and there is also a higher, purer,
deeper insight into Reality. An adult can follow the
thinking of a child, for he has been a child himself;
but he can also understand things which the child is
unable to comprehend. It is better not to explain
this to the child, for the child won't understand – if
he did, his understanding would no longer be childish, but adult. And we, who *can* follow this analogy,
must accept that there could be a higher, spiritual
knowledge which stands to our lower, everyday variety as the adult's understanding does to the child's.
Though of course we shall not thereby acquire this
higher knowledge for ourselves. If we had it we
wouldn't be asking these childish questions all the
time.*

8   This defence cannot be refuted, and it commonly
satisfies the defender very well. But it also prevents
him from preaching, for preaching requires an
audience capable of comprehending what is said.
Those who want to preach – to talk to the 'ignorant', the as-yet-uninitiated, therefore prefer the
third line of defence.

9   On this third view the language of faith can be
understood – to some extent, at least – by any intelligent and interested listener, if only he will make
the right allowances. One has to *learn* to read
poetry, it's no good treating a poem like an instruction manual or a shopping list. One has to learn,
likewise, to say the creed and to appreciate the literature of devotion and discipleship.

10   The terms of the language of faith are not,
then, to be taken in their ordinary sense, but in a
special and qualified way. And the sort of qualification needed in any given case can be worked out, in

principle at least, by the aid of a general theory of this 'special sense', the Theory of Analogy.

11   This third line of defence is the topic of this book.

12   This book – unlike the theory of Analogy – is not defensive in intent. The theory explains how *despite appearances* religious language can be held to make a sort of sense. I shall not be explaining or defending religion on this score. I shall not attack it either. Though I shall present some theories, in a popular sort of way, the book is not meant as a record of old or new discoveries in the logic of theology. It is an account of puzzlements, of points I have tried to understand, and very largely failed.

13   I do not publish these puzzles to make it more difficult for others to believe. I doubt if it would help them if I tried to make it easier. The puzzles are there. They need to be thought through, and solved if possible; or reckoned with, if not.

14   A faith whose profession and exposition is not qualified by an awareness, at least, of the logical and philosophical difficulties which it involves, is less than 'our reasonable service'. There are good and religious reasons for wanting to work out just what sort of nonsense religious talk may be.

15   This 'problem of Analogy' is not, I shall argue, a problem for religion (in the sense of personal faith) so much as for theology. Nor is it a problem only for Christian theology. It arises equally in every variety of theism, and in most non-theistic systems too. It is a problem, we may say, for metaphysics, i.e. for any argumentative theorising about the ultimate nature of our universe. It arises in some of the special sciences of nature too.

16   The scope of this book will clearly be very wide.

But the book is quite short, and the author's learning very limited. The treatment is bound to be superficial. It is only an introduction. It seeks to show that there is a problem here, and that that problem has not yet been solved. Others – the reader, for instance – will have to do the rest.

11. Danger: Parliament at Work

MR GRYLL   While we are on the subject of misnomers, what say you to the wisdom of Parliament?
THE REV. DR OPIMIAN   Why, sir, I do not call that a misnomer. The term wisdom is used in a parliamentary sense. The wisdom of Parliament is a wisdom *sui generis*. It is not like any other wisdom. It is not the wisdom of Socrates, nor the wisdom of Solomon. It is the wisdom of Parliament. It is not easily analysed or defined; but it is very easily understood. It has achieved wonderful things by itself, and still more when Science has come to its aid. Between them they have poisoned the Thames, and killed the fish in the river. A little further development of the same wisdom, and science will complete the poisoning of the air and kill the dwellers on the banks. It is pleasant that the precious effluvium has been brought so efficiently under the Wisdom's own wise nose. Thereat the nose, like Trinculo's, has been in great indignation. The Wisdom has ordered the Science to do something. The Wisdom does not know what, nor the Science either. But the Wisdom has empowered the Science to spend some millions of money; and this, no doubt, the Science will do. When the money has been spent, it will be found that the something has been worse than nothing. The Science will want more money, to do some other something, and the Wisdom will grant it.*

2   How unfair! But you have to be relevant, to be unfair. And this piece seems as relevant today as when it was published, in 1861. So many parliamentary 'improvements' have left things so very much the same . . . But we don't need another tirade. Let us look instead at the reverend Doctor's concept of a special 'parliamentary' sense.

3   Opimian meant, of course, that the 'wisdom of Parliament' was to be taken with a shovelful of salt: that the intellectual and practical character of Parliament's actions was not in fact wisdom at all, but foolishness. To describe the democratic carry-on as *wise* was just parliamentary humbug, a way of calling black white in a sonorous voice in the hope that no one would stop to look at it.

4   The inverted commas around the word *improvements* have a similar effect, warning the reader not to take too seriously what is actually said. Another such signal is an exclamation mark in brackets afterwards:-

> The general said the withdrawal was part of his strategic plan, and its completion was a major victory (!)

The writer reports what the general said, and adds *sotto voce* 'believe that if you can'.

5   Let us call these various devices 'operators', and say that they 'qualify' the terms or expressions to which they are applied – as a £ or $ sign may be said to qualify the numbers that come after it.† And let us ask how these sarcastic operators work.

6   Clearly the operator affects our appreciation of what is being said. But does it alter the meaning of the terms? Does the word *wisdom* mean something different when applied to Parliament? Is *strategic victory* a longer name for 'tactical defeat'?

7   Some say every word has its own proper meaning, and is either used correctly, or abused. When
used incorrectly the word means nothing (in that
context). To qualify is to destroy. This strict and
simple requirement has been grandly called the Postulate of Univocity.

8   On this view humbug is impossible. For humbug
involves the abuse of language, and abuse renders
the language in question meaningless, and then no
one *could* be taken in.

9   Opimian suggests another view: that some
words sometimes bear a special sense. The wisdom
qualified as 'parliamentary' has its meaning thereby
altered, not destroyed. The operator does not dis-
qualify it from meaning anything, but changes its
meaning to something different and unusual. Some
words, on this view, have an extra meaning in addition to their ordinary one.

10 Some words have more than one ordinary
meaning, of course, but that is a different affair. For
example, the word *bank* means a hump of ground, a
row of keys, machines or seats, or a group of money-
lenders who borrow your money to lend out at interest and charge you for the privilege. *Neat* means tidy,
undiluted, or an ox or cow. The dictionary says the
three meanings of *bank* all derive, by a plausible suc-
cession of ideas, from Old Teutonic *bankon*, whereas
neat has two origins, a Latin word for 'shiny' and a
Teutonic root which means 'possess'. But this
makes little difference to our present purposes. In
speaking current English we could, if we like, regard
neat as one word with three meanings. Or, if we
prefer univocity, we could just as well say there are
three distinct words spelt b – a – n – k, and enter
them separately as *bank*[1], *bank*[2] and *bank*[3]. This freedom is still however limited by linguistic facts. It is

not open to us to take 'cow' as a special sense of a word that usually means 'tidy'; nor can we explain *Bank of England* by qualifying our understanding of a hump of ground.

11   While these double and triple meanings do make punning possible, the contexts of the different senses are so different that there is no danger of real misunderstanding through ambiguity. But in the case of a special or qualified sense, such as 'parliamentary wisdom', punning is impossible and ambiguity is rife. Many will take the term at face value, literally. Parliamentarians and others in the know will discount it suitably.

12   At what stage does this 'wisdom' acquire its special sense? For humbug to work the humbugger must appear to use his terms in their proper and ordinary sense. When official spokesmen describe a change for the worse, e.g. from daily to weekly milk delivery, as an 'improvement', their aim is to hoodwink the public into putting up with it. The humbugger's claim must be plausible; if it were nonsense it would not work at all. In the same way an actor must pretend that his actions on stage are 'for real'. A stage fight must contain fighting actions and talk, though the strokes are feints and all the blood is ink. A stage whisper must be made behind the hand, not spoken full face or bellowed through a megaphone.

13   The audience can of course console themselves that 'it's only a play', but if they do so the drama loses its effect. And when Opimian tells us that the 'wisdom of Parliament' is wisdom in a special sense he is rendering the humbug harmless by exposure. If the 'wisdom' is seen as qualified then nobody is taken in.

14   We seem to have reached two contradictory

positions. The term *wisdom* is not meaningless when applied to Parliament, but it does not bear its usual sense, nor has it another ordinary sense (as in the case of *bank*), so it must have a special and parliamentary sense. But if it is taken in this (undetermined) special sense then nothing is served by applying it to Parliament. Either we take it literally and seriously, and are taken in by it; or we see through the humbug, and humorously qualify the 'wisdom' as Parliamentary, after which no one can take it seriously again.

15   Humbug is a form of deceit, of lying. Now a lie does not confer a special negative sense on the terms employed; if that happened, it would be impossible to tell a lie. The words must keep their ordinary sense in order for the sentence to be false. And when someone calls it a lie they do not qualify the meanings of the words in the sentence, but rather tell us how to treat the statement that is made, viz. as a deliberate falsehood intended to mislead.

16   We must now qualify (i.e. alter and correct) something we said earlier. The operator (!) does not affect the meanings of the terms employed so much as the way we 'take' the statement as a whole.† It recommends a pinch of salt. That is why the operator stands outside the sentence, and is not attached to any one term in particular. Now the same is true, though less obvious, for sarcastic inverted commas; they say that *improvement* was what the man called it (– and you know what to make of that!). The same goes for *Parliamentary wisdom*. There is no special, esoteric sense in which we may say that Parliament is wise. *Wise* means wise, but a hint that that's what they call it – the politicians and the judges and the journalists – will do for a nod or a wink to any blind horses who may be listening.

17   There are formal parallels, sometimes uncomfortably close, between the humbug of politics and the rhetoric of religious preachers and apologists. The religion boys say extraordinary things which turn out, on close inspection, not to be literally true; when challenged, they are apt to claim that their terms must be taken in some special sense. The love of God is not like the love of man or wife, of mother or of son. It is a love *sui generis*, all on its own. Prayers are 'answered', not by granting what was asked but by whatever happens being thought of as an answer to the prayer. If the all-caring all-foreseeing leading of Providence lands you in what seems to be a ditch, that must be where you were 'meant' to go; you should sit up and sing 'Lead kindly light' as if it really meant what it actually says. . . .

18   Is the parallel exact? Some say it is, regarding the statements of preachers as straightforward and interested falsehoods, directly comparable to those put about by politicians, advertisers and other quacks. The falsehoods are deliberate, and are meant to be taken literally, as the actions likely to be taken by those who believe them are expected to suit the preacher's pocket or his other purposes. This is one view of the nature of religious talk, and quite a sensible view for anyone who holds (i) that the talk is meant to be taken literally, (ii) that the statements made are false, and (iii) that the preacher himself is not so stupid as to be unaware of this.

19   On another view, the preacher is muddled but sincere. The religious claims he makes are actually nonsensical or false, but he thinks he can make sense of them and believes them to be true. That they are in fact nonsensical can be demonstrated by careful argument from the claims themselves, for

they have some consequences which are mutually contradictory and others which conflict with well-established facts. The preacher's heart is in the right place, but he is not too hot on inference, and simply fails to appreciate the logical implications of his claims. If coherent and true, those claims *would be* of great interest and importance to everyone, so one need not suggest ulterior motives for making them. Logical incompetence is sufficient explanation, and very understandable.

20   Either view assumes that religious talk is meant to be taken literally. On the former view it consists of knowingly making false statements; on the latter, of unintentional falsehood – or nonsense – believed by the speaker to be both good sense and true, and so commended by him, quite commendably, to others for belief.

21   The preacher himself may be puzzled which attack to meet. (By 'preacher' I mean anyone who tries to convey his basic convictions about life to others by means of verbal exposition, whether in the form of narratives, moral appeal or argument). When charged with literal and interested falsehood he will probably insist that his claims are literally true. Shifts and qualifications seem out of place in preaching: they would water down his convictions and weaken the force of his appeal. When faced with a reasoned objection he begins to plead a 'special sense' in which his words are to be taken herebelow; so taken, his claims will appear to the strictest scrutiny both intelligible and compatible with known facts about the world. But when it comes to constructive argument and theological debate the special sense is forgotten once again; the witching hour has passed and everything seems clear and solid in the light of day.

14   DO WE NEED A THEORY OF ANALOGY?

22   Which of these three preachers should we listen to?

III. Analogy and Arguments

THERE is a classic doctrine on this matter, associated with the name of Thomas Aquinas and known as the theory of Analogy. The theory states that some terms which religious people apply to God are not to be taken precisely in their ordinary sense, nor yet in a totally different sense, but in a special and related sense; and that the relationship of this special sense to the ordinary sense can be appreciated by means of a certain 'proportion' or 'ratio' or (to use the Greek term) 'analogy'. The things people say about God, on this view, are not to be taken literally (*univoce* in a single sense), neither are they fatally ambiguous (*equivoce* used in a double sense) – for then their ordinary sense would provide no clue to their religious meaning, and taking them literally would make complete nonsense of what they really meant: rather they are to be taken analogically (*analogice* in a related or appropriate sense), so that a literal acceptance of these religious statements (such as is surely made by those of 'simple faith') is a first step, and a step in the right direction, and will require only correction and qualification, not radical revision in the life-and-death-long progress towards fuller appreciation of the real significance of what is being said.

2   This theory is often stated by formulating a relationship between meanings of terms; between a word (e.g. *love*) used in its everyday sense and the

same word used as a technical term of theology and applied to God. The theory offers to state this relationship in a precise and quasi-mathematical manner, as a correspondence between two ratios:

$$\frac{love \text{ in God}}{love \text{ in man}} \; : \; \frac{\text{being of God}}{\text{being of man}}$$

This appears to be a working formula, a rule of thumb, as if to say 'If you want to understand what it means to speak of God's love, consider ordinary human love and then think of the difference between God and man, and make appropriate allowances'. Human love is only a pale reflection of divine love, but it is a genuine reflection; it gives us some inkling of what God's love must be like.†

3   This theory will be discussed in more detail later on and contrasted with other theories of how religious language comes to bear a 'special but related sense'. Some of these theories apply direct to theological terms; in others it is religious statements as complete units, rather than their linguistically incomplete constituents, that require qualification and interpretation. Some theorists offer to tell you how to make this qualification, as though one should start off with everyday language and then apply an appropriate 'conversion factor' to obtain the corresponding theological significance. For others such a mechanical approach is wholly misguided. Religious meaning cannot be constructed according to a formula; it has to grow on its own, in its own setting in life, and it takes its nature from that soil. But all these theories are concerned with what may be called (in a slightly wider sense) the analogical character of religious or theological language: i.e. with the (supposed) fact that it is to be 'taken' in a *special, proper, appropriate but related* sense.

4   This book will not be much concerned with what is commonly called 'argument by analogy'. The phrase covers a multitude of distinct logical sins, each of which, very likely, some biblical or religious writer could be proven to commit. The same would be true if we considered political writers as a class, or mathematical, or biological. Anyone explaining a difficult and abstract matter to a beginner will have recourse to analogies, i.e. to other things somewhat similar but more familiar; and if argument fails he may rely on the comparison to convince as well as illustrate (see XII, *post*). But that is not directly to our present point. We are not concerned with the way in which while trying to make a religious point the preacher may voluntarily and separately refer to something else that strikes him as somehow similar, but with the extent to which he finds himself forced to take terms from other areas when he attempts a direct, a purely theological expression of his religious point.

5   We shall however be very much concerned with the effect that analogy – the analogical use of terms – has on arguments in theology. Any theory of a 'special sense' has serious consequences for theology as an argumentative science of the divine. For if a term in the premiss of an argument is used in a special sense, we must ensure that it is used in precisely the same sense throughout or the argument will fail for ambiguity; and we need to know what the special sense is, in order to grasp the conclusion properly. A conclusion validly inferred but not fully understood would be like a map drawn by secret conventions: grand to have but no use at all for getting there.

6   It is (to anticipate a little) because of this

difficulty in assessing the effect on theological arguments of a theory of analogy, that preachers and theologians give the impression of adopting it only as a defensive ploy; and this tends to give the theory itself a bad name. People think of it as a form of philosophical casuistry, a learned way of saying that black is near to grey and therefore almost white. Why don't you religious people just say what you mean, then like others you'll be able to mean exactly what you say!

7   I am not concerned to attack or defend theologians on this score, but to get the theories clear. If a theologian appeals at some stage to some theory of analogy, it seems fair to ask him to put it at the beginning of his book. If it saves some of his theses it must presumably apply to all of them. It cannot be Rule 42 in the theological language-game. Provided this is done we may invite the sceptic – on the same grounds of fairness – not to assume *before* hearing it that any theory of special meanings is a form of special pleading or humbug. After hearing, we must all think what we can.

8   Preachers are not of course the only people to 'borrow' terms from other areas. To look no further than the present paragraph, *borrowing* is a term borrowed from the money market; the notion of *fields* or *areas* is taken from land-surveying; and a *term* is properly an end, as in *bus terminus*. We may if we wish to be very strict describe all these as metaphors, provided we remember that the term *metaphor* is itself a metaphor.*

9   Even if these examples are dismissed as mere etymology, irrelevant to the present and proper meanings of the terms, there are still plenty of cases where people have to get along with borrowed terms, on a never-never basis, with little prospect of

converting the loan to real ownership. We speak of a 'current' of electricity, of the 'faculties' of mind and will, of a 'swing' in voting and of 'inflation' in the economy (see XVI, *post*). A satisfactory theory of analogy should either be general enough to apply to these cases too or else should show good cause why religion is such a *special* special case.

10 Our discussion will be general in another way as well. We shall have to consider some topics in what may be called the logic of terms; whether it is words or terms that we define, whether definition can create a meaning or only circumscribe it, whether everyone is free to define as they please, whether a good definition must assign some set of features common to all the proper uses of the term and so constituting its essential meaning (see XIV, XV, *post*). These are matters of some dispute among those who trouble with such things, quite apart from questions about religious language. They may be of little apparent interest to those who do worry about religious language but who do not care for tussles in philosophy. But they must be considered if we are to deal with our problem properly.

11 The problem of how to take religious language is I believe common to all religions, and our discussion is therefore meant to apply to all of them. But my own experience is very limited. I have not professed many religions yet. Most of my examples will in consequence refer to Christianity, and more particularly to certain forms of Protestant Christianity current in this country in the twentieth century. That is a very restricted basis for generalisation, almost as restricted as the astronomer's or the geologist's. One can get along at all in such cases only by assuming that instances of which one has not had direct experience will be similar in relevant

ways to those that one has come across: that things
and people are reasonably regular. Readers familiar
with the same little corner of religion may be interested in what I say: perhaps those who know
another corner will be kind enough to correct me
where a generalising habit has led me to say something untrue to their experience.

12   There is another limitation to be considered at
the outset. This work is meant to be one of abstract
and impartial philosophical analysis. It has as its
field certain logical facts or relations of ideas. It is
possible to state these facts correctly, or to get them
muddled up. Ideally, the judgement as to whether
they are muddled or got straight is an objective one,
uninfluenced by the judge's own philosophical position on other matters. And ideally we should be able
to keep these analytic questions quite distinct from
religious disputes, in which objectivity is not even
usually an aim. But in practice things are rather different. Apart from the difficulty in being philosophically objective – i.e. in not letting one's views
on other matters interfere with one's judgement on
the point under analysis – it is very difficult to separate the philosophical issues from religious ones. (See
XIV.20, *post*)

13   To illustrate this point, consider an obvious initial objection to the programme of enquiry proposed
in this book. 'Why (it may be asked) kick up all this
dust about religious terminology? Theologians may
have their technical terms, but preachers and teachers use ordinary language, and mean exactly what
they say. They teach the faith "once delivered to the
saints", and they need no philosophical theories or
logical apologies for doing so. A few intellectuals
who have lost or mislaid their faith may try to quiet
their consciences by explaining away the creed in a

haze of qualifications and re-definitions. The plain truth is that they are not Christians, and that their complex reformulated non-faith is not Christianity'.

14   Note first that this objection does not undercut the enquiry here proposed; it takes one side in the debate and tries to shout the others down. And it does this for a religious reason. The objector finds the discussion too disturbing to his own faith, and excuses himself from reflecting on it by denying the name of Christian to those who disagree with him. Philosophical analysis may have religious consequences, just as a religious re-formulation may be presented in philosophic guise. It is very difficult to keep them separate.

15   Looking around at twentieth-century Protestant Christianity we can give a concrete reply to this initial objection. It is just not true today that everyone except philosophers accepts religious statements in their ordinary sense. It would be nearer the truth, in our society, to say that the ordinary man does not take them in any sense at all. He is so used to the idea of church as a special sort of place in which rather special people say special things in a very special sort of voice that he rarely attends to anything they say. It is not just that these things have lost their challenge through familiarity. He has an automatic and implicit conviction that religious speakers really don't mean what they say. An adult in our society knows well enough how to treat an election address, or a label saying 'threepence off'. And once he has grasped that it's a parson speaking, or that what he is singing is a hymn, he simply 'switches off'.

16   Everyone has his own idea of the 'ordinary man', so arguments from what he would think are of dubious effect. Less abstract is the 'ordinary

churchgoer', for the teaching he receives can be traced in publications or verified any Sunday evening in a pew. And it soon becomes clear that a literal assent is expected to only some of the statements of the creed. That Jesus sits on God's right hand is a figure of speech for most of those in Sunday School. That he descended into hell was in some earlier centuries thought to denote vertical motion to another place, but is now held to refer (at most) to a non-spatial state, or more commonly to be a way of saying that those born before Jesus were not to be left out. The ascension into heaven is taken literally by some, and by others to mean that after the Resurrection appearances communion with the Lord became purely spiritual. Some people think angels have wings and devils tails; some are surer of angels than devils but less sure of these appendages; some take them all as just a way of speaking of God's traffic with the soul.* And so one could go on. If all Christians take all doctrinal statements literally then there are very few Christians today and not many in any earlier age. This book is about the wider group who only call themselves Christians and prefer to think about their faith.

2. The Theory in Outline

IV. Meaning What We Say

AT LEAST some of the things people say about God will have to be 'taken' in a special sense. That seems clear just from listening. Moreover there are many statements in the literature to this effect. Spiritual things, it is said, must be understood spiritually. A flat, literal acceptance of the sayings of saints would take all the life and goodness out of them.

2 This means, if we take it seriously, that statements about God must acquire a second meaning in addition to their ordinary or superficial one. And *this* is meant quite literally. It is not just that some religious statements, for example those made in acts of worship, take on for that moment a more profound significance, or are brought nearer home to one. It is rather that what the statements have to say undergoes a change. To spell this right out:

> For any religious statement there will be a common-or-garden apparent meaning, x, obtained by ordinary rules of construction and usage, and also a second and special religious (and real) meaning, y.

It may be that y cannot be grasped except by first understanding x. But anyone who takes x to be what the statement really means has failed to catch what the man who made it was really driving at.

3 One way for a statement to acquire a regular and proper second sense is for the terms composing

it to be altered in some way. They must be 'qualified'. We often think of qualification as something
that happens to people; and it is commonly thought
that religious teachers must be specially endowed,
consecrated or inspired, and that religious learners –
those who genuinely 'hear' what the teachers say –
also require some special aptitude or gift or attitude.
But religious communication, on the present theory,
does not only involve, and to some extent require,
changes in the people who communicate, but also in
the meanings of the terms that they employ. The
words of ordinary human language must be adapted
and accommodated to these very superior and special purposes.

4   Some say we could know *a priori* – before listening – that religious statements are to be taken in a
special sense, for the point can be established by
abstract argument. God, it is argued, is infinite and
perfect every way, whereas the world we live in is
imperfect and very limited. We are part of that
world, and share its limitations, and it is on our experience of that world that all our knowledge and
ideas are originally based. Human thought therefore
is finite and imperfect too; a difficulty when it concerns some worldly object, but a fatal flaw when
humans think about the infinite, the all-perfect, the
divine. Here their conceptions must have an intrin-
sic inadequacy. God *cannot* be comprehended properly in ordinary human terms.

5   This argument depends, like most arguments,
on a number of further assumptions that are not
explicitly stated but do need to be examined independently. It seems to use the terms *finite* and *imperfect* interchangeably. But there is nothing imperfect
about the number 3. It seems to assume that a limited being must have limited ideas, whatever that may

mean; and that the idea of something infinite would itself be infinite, though the idea of an elephant is not a grey idea and that of a mile is neither long nor short.

6 Despite all these questionable assumptions, most theists find the argument quite plausible. That men are finite seems undeniable. And the steps from here to the conclusion, that human ideas of infinity must be inadequate, seem natural if not quite unavoidable. Moreover, every sincerely religious man *feels* that whatever he says about God is bound to be unsatisfactory and incomplete. As an Isaiah once tried to put it on behalf of God,

> My thoughts are not your thoughts,
> Neither are your ways my ways, saith the Lord.
> For as the heavens are higher than the earth,
> So are my ways higher than your ways,
> And my thoughts than your thoughts.*

Though that way of putting it is, of course, inadequate.

7 It is sometimes suggested that the argument from human finitude is valid, but only for those who already believe in God. This is not a happy way of putting it. *Selective validity* is a notion unrecognised in logic-books; not because logicians are out of date, or are given to thinking horizontally, or are unable to cope with something so profound, but simply because the notion makes no sense. A valid argument is one that holds good for everyone.

8 It is of course true that not everyone need accept the premisses. Those who reject them can reject the conclusion too. But that would not restrict the argument to theists, for the premisses do not include the statement 'God exists'. An agnostic might very well agree that God (if there is one) is infinite and so

beyond our thought. It is also true that someone
who had no interest at all in the question of God,
and who never came across statements of theology,
might pay no attention to the argument, as a banker
might well disregard the theorem of Pythagoras. But
the banker's disregard would not affect the validity
of Pythagoras' argument.

9   The question whether religious or theological
statements are intrinsically inadequate is of interest
to those who are wondering about God – whether
there really is one and what he must be like – as well
as to their would-be answerers, the theologians. We
may (if we have the nerve) try to divide this group
into believers and unbelievers, but we cannot say
that the argument should be more convincing to
those on one side or other of this line. The plain fact
is that the argument is bad. It *ought not* to convince
anyone. People who take God seriously but are not
too careful in their reasoning tend to welcome the
argument because they feel its conclusion to be true.
And so they recite it from time to time, not so much
to persuade others as to remind themselves, when
taking off on speculative flights, that in their hearts
they know they don't know what they're on about.

10   But if they don't know, then what's the good of
going on? A very pertinent question, and one constantly pressed by the opponents of all religious talk,
and as constantly shirked, they feel, by its apologists. Theology, these opponents say, is just cheat-
ing with words. If you admit to using words in an
extra special sense you are really saying that you
don't mean anything.

11   This objection assumes that every word has a
single proper sense and can be correctly and effect-
ively used only in that sense: a tenet described by its
devotees as the Postulate of Univocity. Stated like

this the maxim seems evidently false, for some words bear several senses, all equally correct. We could of course decide to treat each distinct sense as a separate word. This would make dictionaries longer (and narrower), but might be worth it if it made them clearer too. But in fact it would make some things much more obscure. Consider these entries:

content = 1 what is contained: 2 satisfied.
continent = 1 temperate; 2 mainland.
contingent = 1 accidental; 2 part of an army.
contract = 1 agreement; 2 make or become smaller.

Making these four entries into eight would actually reduce the information they contain, for there are important links between the two senses in each word. A clear path of meaning can be traced from one to the other, by means of a number of usages which fall between. The senses of a word often resemble a continuum, for between any two however close it seems always possible – if we are ready for nice distinctions – to interpolate a third. It is these intermediate senses that defeat any programme for having a single sense to every word simply by making a different word out of every sense.
12   Words are all the time growing new senses, bit by bit, as individual users and linguistic groups stretch their current meanings to cover new cases or to point a similarity. In the last year or two *renege* has become quite popular for *go back on one's word*, a sense nearly but not quite recognised in the Concise Oxford Dictionary:

renege = (cards) revoke; *(archaic)* deny, renounce, abandon.

Hardware has come to mean *gadgetry* in the computer

industry, though no one had previously applied it to machines, and the new term has generated its own opposite, *software*, an entirely new word, for programmes and ways of preparing them. *Hardcore* used to mean *bits of brick and stone* (used in foundations for a road or wall); then someone applied it to rebels who were both determined and irreconcilable, and now we have *softcore* for their more politic comrades, killing off the original metaphor (of a fruit or nut) and suggesting that those who negotiate are not quite right in the head. And in quite another century the Greek words for *assembly* and *good news* rapidly acquired a technical meaning for the members of the latest sect.† We may say all these usages are incorrect. So they are, to begin with. More people take them on, and they win a place in history and in the lexicon, and then it's no good disliking them. These constant little changes and developments are why we say some languages are 'living'. There is no hope of tidying everything up into dictionaries until the language is quite dead.

13   If poets and journalists can stretch the language to their purposes, why should not preachers do the same? The mystic, stumbling to describe his visionary God, will say the most unusual things and his hearers must make what sense they can of it, just as a poet may make his readers labour and puzzle over his intent. Each of these, we may say, has a private meaning which only some of his readers can discern. May we not say the same of a preacher whose sermon 'comes home' to a single member of his audience? – that his words of God had a private meaning which went to the heart of a single individual. He had ears. Who are we, the unaffected, to declare that he could not have heard?

14   There are two rather different cases to be distinguished here. The sermon, we may suppose, was equally *intelligible* to all the audience. The preacher did not use words in an unusual sense. Each of his hearers could have paraphrased any of his sentences. It was the total effect that varied, as it will in any audience. One man accepted his urgings and saw the whole world, and himself, in a novel light. The next man had heard it all before. A third thought the argument was bad. A fourth was finding the seat a bit hard and wondering how long it was to lunch. . . But this variation in effect was not due to the varying meaning or acceptation of the preacher's terms.

15   With the poet and the visionary it is the words themselves that sometimes seem to undergo a change. Here the outsider is quite at a loss. He must find some insider – the poet, or someone else in tune with him – to interpret the mystical words. But if the interpreter succeeds, if he can supply a translation, then the outsider has become an insider, at least for that vision or that poem.

16   There is no denying people's right to use words in any way they please. The question is, whether they mean anything; and that comes down to this question: Can others be enabled to follow what they say? Alice found this very difficult:

    '. . . There's glory for you!'
    'I don't know what you mean by "glory",' Alice said.
    Humpty Dumpty smiled contemptuously. 'Of course you don't – till I tell you. I meant "there's a nice knock-down argument for you." '
    'But "glory" doesn't mean "a nice knock-down argument",' Alice objected.

'When *I* use a word,' Humpty Dumpty said in rather a scornful tone, 'it means just what I choose it to mean – neither more nor less'.

'The question is', said Alice, 'whether you *can* make words mean different things'.

'The question is', said Humpty Dumpty, 'which is to be master – that's all'.

Alice was too much puzzled to say anything, so after a minute Humpty Dumpty began again. 'They've a temper, some of them – particularly verbs, they're the proudest – adjectives you can do anything with, but not verbs – however *I* can manage the whole lot! Impenetrability! That's what *I* say!'

'Would you tell me, please', said Alice, 'what that means?'

'Now you talk like a reasonable child', said Humpty Dumpty, looking very much pleased. 'I meant by "impenetrability" that we've had enough of that subject, and it would be just as well if you'd mention what you mean to do next, as I suppose you don't intend to stop here all the rest of your life'.

'That's a great deal to make one word mean', Alice said in a thoughtful tone.*

17   Some take this as a tale against those who define new terms. Mathematicians, for instance, tend to say things like

Let a plane quadrilateral with parallel sides be called a *parallelogram*,

and expect their readers to accept this new monstrosity. And accept it they must, if they want to read further in that book. They can always look round later for a better word, if they want to use the concept so defined; or they can drop both concept and word, if they have no need for them.* But they cannot complain that the author failed to make his meaning clear. And this is what Alice did complain.

18 When Humpty Dumpty misused (as we would say) the word *glory* Alice was puzzled, not confused. She just had no idea what he meant. Once he had explained that he was just now using it to mean 'there's a nice knock-down argument for you', Alice had no puzzle left, though she might still get confused by trying to take a well-known word in a sense distant, complex, and unfamiliar.

19 Definition by stipulation is not an arbitrary power used by some speakers to impose their terms on us, but a public institution for the defence of our linguistic currency. Under this convention any hearer may challenge a speaker to define his terms, and require him to stick thereafter to the sense defined. The definition itself must be in common terms already understood. The convention thus has the effect of allowing new developments while keeping the meaning fully convertible into old terms that everyone can pass around.*

20 A word may have many meanings, and no harm come of it, if only each of them can be defined. The result of such a definition is a term, a word tied down and restricted to a single meaning clearly delimited. It is to such terms, not to words, that the Postulate of Univocity applies (see XV *post*). It simply demands that each term (word-or-phrase-as-defined) be kept strictly to its defined sense until further notice; that is, until we feel like a change, and re-define.

21 The religious teacher need not, on this view, apologise for using words in a special sense: even heathen and publicans do that. But he

must give some account of them. And that's
where the difficulties start.

22   According to one party the absence of satisfactory definitions for religious terms shows that they
do not after all bear any special sense. And since
they do not, by common confession, bear their
ordinary sense either, they do not bear any sense.
Those who use them are just talking nonsense in a
solemn voice. *Nonsensicalism* seems a fair name for
this theory.

23   On another view, also mentioned above, there
is a special sense but it has to be perceived by individuals and cannot be publicly defined. This makes
theology quite mysterious, so we may call it *Mysticalism*.

24   It is against Mysticalism that the Humpty
Dumpty story really tells. Until he explains his
usage Alice has – and can have – no idea what he
intends. Suppose he had refused to explain, and just
left her to catch up. If she ever did, her new understanding of *glory* and *impenetrability* would be evident, to herself or to others, only from her being
able to explain. It is the possibility of explaining, to
oneself or another, that shows we have a meaning
for the term. If Humpty Dumpty could not explain
himself even to himself we should have to say that
he did not know what he was talking about.

25   Language is public. It is a vehicle for communication from one to another. A private, indefinable, 'mystical' language would not be a language
at all. It might have other significances, but it
would be meaningless. Mysticalism is Nonsensicalism in prophetic garb.

26   The alternative is to formulate a theory of the
religious use of terms. Such a theory must explain
just how special is the sense that they acquire in

religious use, and it must show how to 'construct' that meaning from their ordinary sense: not that all must or indeed any would learn the meaning in that way, but just to show that a definition is possible 'in principle'. One such theory is Aquinas' Theory of Analogy.

V. Saying What We Mean

UNIVOCITY in theology – calling God *strong* or *sensible* and meaning just exactly that – would lead to anthropomorphism, to making God in the image of a Mr Jones. And anthropomorphism is anathema. But equivocation – calling God *good* or *great* but not really meaning anything like that – is also unacceptable, for it makes complete nonsense of theology. Is there a third alternative?

2 As a way between ignorant literalism and literal ignorance it is proposed that theological terms be taken in a *different but related sense*. God is called *strong*, on this view, not quite in the way that a man or a horse is so described, nor yet in some quite novel and unintelligible way, but in a way proportioned to his divine nature. God is 'strong' in a way appropriate to God.

3 This is not to say that God is strong*er*, as a horse is stronger than a man. For the horse's strength, *as strength*, is just the same as man's; it's just that there is more of it. If *it* weren't the same there couldn't be more *of it*. Difference of degree presupposes identity of quality. Now God's strength, we are trying to say, is different in quality. He is not just simply strong, as we understand strength, but 'strong' in his own inimitable way.

4 Very inimitable, you may say. For how can anything come between *being the same* and *being different*? If A is not the same as B, that makes it different. If B

were not different from A, it would have to be the
same. It must take a very thin angel, a real pin-
balancer, to get between dissimilarity and identity.

5   That is not entirely fair. Theological predica-
tion, it was admitted, is really different from the
ordinary sort. Terms just do not mean the same
when they are applied to God. But there are degrees
and sorts of *difference*. It was only denied that terms
acquire an entirely new sense when brought into
theology. Their meaning is not wholly different. It is
related to their ordinary sense; and if we start from
the ordinary sense (as we must) we can gain some
understanding of what is being said.

6   Can we state the relationship? Can we say in
general how different a theological term will be, in
significance, from its ordinary use? There is a classic
formula for this, though there is also much dispute
as to what it means and how it can be used. Taking
'strength' as the term, the formula runs:

$$\frac{\text{'strength' in God}}{\text{nature of God}} :: \frac{\text{strength (in man)}}{\text{human nature}}$$

It is usual to add that this is not an equation but a
ratio of relationships. In mathematics this distinction would make little difference; for if we consider
two similar triangles with sides a, b, c and x, y, z, we
can say either

$$a \text{ is to } b \text{ as } x \text{ is to } y$$

stating a similarity of relationships: or, equally well,
we may say

$$\frac{a}{b} = \frac{x}{y}$$

stating the same facts as an equality of ratios.

7   Let us take the mathematical interpretation one

stage further. If the ratios are treated like fractions we can multiply across, going from

$$\frac{a}{b} = \frac{x}{y}$$

to

$$a = b \cdot \frac{x}{y}$$

and so to

$$a = x \cdot \frac{b}{y}$$

This suggests a similar move from our original statement

$$\frac{\text{'strength' in God}}{\text{nature of God}} :: \frac{\text{strength (in man)}}{\text{human nature}}$$

to

$$\frac{\text{'strength'}}{\text{in God}} = \frac{\text{strength}}{\text{(in man)}} \times \frac{\text{nature of God}}{\text{human nature}}$$

That is to say, the term 'strong' when applied to God must be qualified by the (infinite) difference between God and man. To discover the real meaning of God's almighty power we must take ordinary human strength and 'multiply' it by this difference. God's strength really is strength, but of a sort appropriate to God. He is strong in his own inimitable way.

8   These re-arrangements of the formula suggest that it might be used to show just how different a meaning the term acquires when applied to God. And it would certainly be convenient to have a 'conversion factor' ready when studying religious utterance – as an Englishman reading a French novel might be glad of a rule of thumb for changing Centigrade to Fahrenheit or kilometres into miles. For theological use we just 'multiply' the given term by

the difference between man and God. It is a big difference of course; the calculation may be astronomical, but no doubt the professionals get quite handy at making the appropriate allowances.

9   Do we know the difference? Yes and No. We can frame definitions readily enough. By 'man' we mean a rational animal, a member of the species *homo sapiens*. By 'God' we refer to an infinite eternal and self-existent being who is responsible for everything. And the contrast between these two definitions is certainly significant, for it supplied the main reason for refusing to take theological terms literally and univocally. But a definition affords only an outline and referential knowledge of the thing defined. Its primary function is to explain what we do (and do not) mean by a certain term. We cannot extract from it more knowledge than we were able to put in. So the question is, how far do we know the 'natures', the being, of man or of God?

10   As to human nature our present knowledge is far from adequate. No doubt policemen and priests know better than most 'what is in man', what his capabilities are for deeds and plans both mean and great. But that is because they have a more varied experience 'of life' as we say, i.e. of men. Even their knowledge does not go much beyond their personal experience. And if psychology should one day become a science it would not explain altogether what man is and can be, but only how his mind and personality grow and operate.

11   There is nevertheless a clear sense in which each of us knows sufficiently well what human nature is. We may not be able to furnish a full theoretical account of man, but we do know what it is like in practice being one. So we know what 'strength' is when applied to man, for we can see its

relation to human nature in everyday experience.
12   This personal, practical view of the matter is
presumably lacking in our ideas about God. We
have an outline knowledge of his nature, from the
definition; we can explain in general terms ('eternal', 'self-subsistent') what we mean (and do not
mean) by 'God'. But these terms do not show what
precise allowances will have to be made when we
call him 'strong'. What sort of strength is appropriate to an infinite and eternal being? We simply
do not know, for we have no experience to go upon.
We don't know what it is like to be God so we
cannot say what sort of allowances would be appropriate.
13   The 'equation' then contains not one but two
unknowns. It is insoluble. It does not enable us to
work out what 'strength' must be in God, but only
to indicate the direction of our ignorance when we
use that term of him. It says that God's strength is of
a very special sort, and that no one but God can possibly tell what that special sort must be. God *is*
strong (we shall now say this twice as loud) but in a
way inimitable by us and (*sotto voce*) unknown and
indescribable.
14   Some will say this agnostic conclusion results
from taking the mathematical comparison too literally. The notion of a 'conversion factor' is surely too
mechanical, like applying a slide-rule to the interpretation of Shakespeare.

> The business man who assumes that this life is
> everything, and the mystic who asserts that it is
> nothing, fail, on this side and on that, to hit the
> truth. 'Yes, I see, dear; it's about half-way be-
> tween,' Aunt Juley had hazarded in earlier years.
> No; truth, being alive, was not half-way between

anything. It was only to be found by continuous excursions into either realm, and though proportion is the final secret, to espouse it at the outset is to ensure sterility.*

There is no hope that handy formulae will save labour in the search for truth; and they do not seem to help much in the search for understanding in theology. For the equation from which we started is not a real equation, but only a comparison, an illustrative analogy.

15   Perhaps no one since Pythagoras has really supposed that God is a number or any sort of quantity. And only a quantity or number can figure in an equation or form part of a ratio. It is not just that the half (say) *of some number* must be another number; for that would leave it possible that my love or strength or intelligence is half of yours. It is rather that if any one thing, X, is *half* of some other thing, Y, then both X and Y must be numbers or quantities or things that can properly be ranked alongside and measured by numbers and other quantities. So it seems simply silly to talk about ratios or proportions between God's nature and his strength. What is not quantified cannot be proportional.

16   If the 'equation' is not to be taken literally, i.e. mathematically, then how are we to take it? Can we not explain in other and proper terms the point that this mathematical comparison was supposed to illustrate? An analogy that leads only to denials looks a bit too theological!

17   It is sometimes possible to say how things are in a quite general way without claiming to know in any detail how they will be in particular. And such a statement can have its uses for those whose

interest is theoretical. Take for instance Aristotle's
suggestion that virtue is a sort of mean or average.
That is, you can always have too much of a good
thing; and having too little is also possible in every
case. This does not tell us how much of the good
would be the right amount, in any given case. For
example, it does not say how much courage, and on
what occasions, would add up to bravery. It only
says that while one can have too little (cowardice)
one could also have too much (foolhardiness).
Whatever the virtue in question, this theory says
that we can either overshoot or undershoot the
mark.* Now this statement is formal and theoretical: we cannot use it to work out our duty in any
given case. But it is not quite empty, all the same;
for there *might* have been good of which it was impossible to have too much, and the theory says that
this is not the case.

18   The comparison suggested in the so-called
'equation' of proportion or analogy may also be
taken in this purely formal and general way. It is no
surprise in that case that we cannot use it to work
out the precise meaning of any particular term we
may apply to God. All it says is that the theological
meaning, when grasped, will be found to stand to
the ordinary meaning in the way God stands to
man. We can't say offhand, nor can we calculate,
just what is the 'different but related' sense borne by
a term in theology; but we can say in advance that
that sense (whatever it is) will be *appropriate*.

19   Put like this, the theory of analogy simply re-
states the original point that God is so different from
man that our language must also become different
when applied to him. But it does not say how different. So taken, the theory is quite agnostic in effect. It
says that no one can know what he is saying when

talking about God. But before we explore the further consequences of this understanding of the theory let us briefly consider some related points commonly made in expositions of the theory.

3. Some Details of the Theory

VI. What Elephants Aren't

Is *everything* that is said about God said in theologians' code? Or are some basic and simple things sayable' in clear'? If so, can enough be made out to show us where to find the key? – or at least, to confirm that believers are not just gabbling when they go on in their code?

2   A great many things may be literally denied of the divine. God, we may say with some assurance, is not a thing, nor a fish or a bird or a beast, nor even like a man. He has no address where we could visit him. He is not six, or five, or ten feet tall. He does not go to sleep. He has no special friends or personal enemies. He never gets excited or fed up. . . .*

3   We seem to be saying quite a lot, in this negative way. Is it possible that if we went on long enough like this we could reach a conclusion that is positive?

4   The 'way of denial' or 'taking away' (*via remotionis*) was first explored in the West by the Neo-Platonists of the fifth century A.D. They took very seriously the argument from human finitude: that people, whose knowledge is based on earthly forms and things, cannot say anything positive about a Being so completely different. All one can do, they inferred, is to go round denying the million and one things that are not to be compared with ***.

5   Research of this sort was said to lead to 'nescience' or ignorance. In some cases this would be

progress, though of a negative variety. Anyone given to thinking of God as a tree or a number or a horse can have his ideas improved by denial, by removing these false and inadequate ideas of the divine.

6   The Neo-Platonist writer known to us, appropriately, as *not* the Dionysius converted by St. Paul*, tried to list what God is not:

> Unto this darkness which is beyond light we pray that we may come, and attain unto vision through the loss of sight and knowledge, and that in ceasing thus to see or to know we may learn to know that which is beyond all perception and understanding (for this emptying of our faculties is true sight and knowledge), and that we may offer him that transcends all things the praises of a transcendent hymnody, which we shall do by denying or removing all things that are – like as men who, carving a statue out of marble, remove all the impediments that hinder the clear perspective of the latent image and by this mere removal display the hidden statue itself in its hidden beauty.... We therefore maintain that the universal cause transcending all things is neither impersonal nor lifeless nor without understanding: in short, that it is not a material body, and therefore does not possess outward shape or intelligible form, or quality, or quantity, or solid weight; nor has it any local existence which can be perceived by sight or touch; nor has it power of perceiving or being perceived; nor does it suffer any vexation or disorder of earthly passions, or any feebleness through the tyranny of material chances, or any want of light; nor any change, or decay, or division, or deprivation, or ebb and flow, or anything else

which the senses can perceive. None of these things can be either identified with it or attributed to it.

Once more, ascending yet higher we maintain that it is not soul, or mind, or endowed with the faculty of imagination, conjecture, reason or understanding; nor is it any act of reason or understanding; nor can it be described by the reason or perceived by the understanding, since it is not number, or order, or greatness, or littleness, or equality, or inequality, and since it is not immovable nor in motion, or at rest, and has no power, and is not power or light, and does not live, and is not life; nor is it personal essence, or eternity, or time; nor can it be grasped by the understanding, since it is not knowledge or truth; nor is it kingship or wisdom; nor is it one, nor is it unity, nor is it Godhead or goodness; nor is it a Spirit, as we understand the term, since it is not Sonship or Fatherhood; nor is it any other thing such as we or any other being can have knowledge of; nor does it belong to the category of non-existence or to that of existence; nor do existent beings know it as it actually is, nor does it know them as they actually are; nor can reason attain to it to name it or know it; nor is it darkness, nor is it light, or error, or truth; nor can any affirmation or negation apply to it; for while applying affirmations or negations to those orders of being that come next to it, we apply not unto it either affirmation or negation, inasmuch as it transcends all affirmation by being the perfect and unique cause of all things, and transcends all negation by the pre-eminence of its simple and absolute nature – free from every limitation and beyond them all*.

7   Can such denials ever add to our knowledge? Do they make any positive contribution to theology? Thomas thought they might:

> By its immensity the divine substance surpasses every form that our intellect reaches. Thus we are unable to apprehend it by knowing *what it is*. Yet we are able to have some knowledge of it by knowing *what it is not*. Furthermore we approach nearer to God according as through our intellect we are able to remove more and more things from him. For we know each thing more perfectly the more fully we see its differences from other things. . . . . (as) in the case of things whose definitions we know. We locate them in a genus, through which we know in a general way what they are. Then we add differences to each thing, by which it may be distinguished from other things. . . . (but) we must derive the distinction of God from other beings by means of negative differences. . . . (and) one negative difference is contracted by another that makes it to differ from many beings. For example, if we say that God is not an accident, we thereby distinguish him from all accidents. Then, if we add that he is not a body, we shall further distinguish him from certain substances. And thus, proceeding in order, by such negations God will be distinguished from all that he is not.*

8   This seems to suggest that each consecutive denial takes us a little further along the road to God; for if we were to succeed in ruling out everything that he is not we should surely be left only with what he *is*.

9   To proceed by elimination in this way we should first of all need to know *all* the things, of which all but one are to be denied: and we should also need to

know that they are *all* the things. Clearly we have no such handy check-list of the items in the universe. Aquinas however does not suggest an elimination item by item, but by sorts. We are not to deny the equivalence with God of particular objects or individuals (this tree, John Smith, that horse); we are to say in some systematic way that God is not this or that sort or type of thing (such as man, tree or animal). The list of such categories is probably finite and may (with luck) be relatively short. Even so, can a series of 'negative differences' leave us with a conception of what God positively *is*?

10   An ordinary, positive difference is a property peculiar to the thing defined: thus we mark off *man* from all the other members of his family, *animal*, by saying that he, and only he, is *rational*. A negative difference, presumably, is a property common to other things but *peculiarly absent* from the thing defined, as *having a motor* is common to many different vehicles and absent, peculiarly, from bicycles.

11   How would such negative differences function in practice? Let us take as example the child's catch-question, What is the difference between an elephant and a pillar-box?† We can answer, of course, but we hardly know where to start. We can say that an elephant is neither red nor hollow, metallic nor cylindrical; that pillar-boxes have no legs or tusks or trunks and are not popularly thought to harbour injuries. But the first list of negative differences would not, however long we went on, convey to any third party the notion of an elephant, nor would the second make anyone think of 'pillar-box'. The negative definition can begin. It can go on indefinitely. But it can never do its job.

12   For another illustration think of the game 'Animal, Vegetable or Mineral?' Here I try to guess

what you are thinking of by suggesting types of thing to which it could belong. From your affirmative answers I gradually narrow down the field until I am able to guess the actual item that you have in mind. Now suppose we played this in the negative, asking always 'Is it *un*like so-and-so?'. Affirmative answers would get us nowhere pretty fast. For by learning that *y* is unlike *x* we make only negative progress in the discovery of *y*.

13   It may be said that these examples are unfair, because their effect is really circular; that the deficiencies of negative definition cannot be coherently demonstrated by exhibiting tasks that it fails to achieve. Let us try a more positive approach. Take marriage – a very positive affair, according to many of its practitioners – and consider how a married person differs in practice from a celibate. Marriage may be defined, negatively, as an undertaking to keep off the others: off other women, for the man; for the woman, other men. How does this 'forsaking all other' differ from celibacy? Well, a celibate is someone determined simply to keep off: for a man, to keep off women; for a woman, men. Now – to make our example even more concrete and specific and positive – let us think of one particular man, called George, inhabiting a town of some 300,000 souls. Is he celibate? Then there are (in round figures) 100,000 women about for him to keep off. Is he married? That reduces the number to 99,999. But this reduction is statistically insignificant. For one thing, the population of women goes up whenever one turns up on a bus from somewhere else. George's celibacy, negatively defined, would in any fair-sized town be practically indistinguishable from his married state.

14   It is hardly surprising that the way of denial

yields no positive knowledge of God, or of marriage, or an elephant. But a positive knowledge of God, say some, is not to be expected herebelow. As Aquinas puts it (at the end of the passage quoted earlier)

> Finally, there will then be a proper consideration of God's substance when he will be known as distinct from all things. Yet this knowledge will not be perfect, since it will not tell us what God is in himself.*

15   We can know about God only that he is, and is beyond our ken, and is responsible for all the things we know. We cannot tell anyone what he is like, for if we knew we could not state it even to ourselves. This view reappears in Kant, but applied to Things-in-General, or The Universe. We can know it or them, he says, only in the way in which they appear to our minds, not as they really are quite apart from our thought of them. But we can know that they (or it) exist, for there must be some real nature-of-things, otherwise how could there be appearances or phenomena of them for us to observe? The *Ding-an-Sich* (thing-as-it-really-is) is there, and is known to be there, yet it is positively unknowable, i.e. it cannot be any further and reliably described. All we can say about it is that it is (or may be) different from phenomena, and (if so) is responsible for them.*

16   Will the way of denial get us anywhere? That depends where we are when we begin. To a plain ordinary man it will furnish plenty of undeniable and useless truths about the Absolute, without yielding real insight or allowing him really to *say* anything. Those previously lucky, however, may here be more fortunate. For someone already acquainted, in some unspeakable way, with that

ineffable *** whose nature the negative theologian is so signally failing to describe may possibly gather from his nods and winks and headshakings that it's You-Know-What he's on about. It may indeed be, as a modern writer claims, that theological burbling can help a penny drop;† but only, one would think, for those already fitted with the right shaped slot. And even they cannot tell us which penny dropped or where it went. The burbling cannot humanly convey positive and public meaning to those not already 'in the know'.

17   Now religious people have not in fact usually thought of God as wholly Other than themselves,† or as totally ineffable. They have had many positive and some surprising things to say about him, and they have insisted on saying these things to the unconverted, i.e. to those who supposedly are *not* already in the know. To justify their practice we need a theory of religious language which will guarantee positive and generally intelligible meaning to at least some statements about God.

18   Will the theory of Analogy meet this need? All it has done so far, on our showing, is explain that there is a need. Things said about God (it says) are to be taken in a special, theological sense. So far so bad. Is there any hope of our discovering what sense that is?

VII. What We Can't Say Clearer

EDWYN BEVAN distinguishes two types of religious symbol:

There are the symbols behind which we can see and the symbols behind which we cannot see. By the symbols behind which we can see I mean those which represent an idea which we seem to discern in a way enabling us to express it in other terms more truly. When, for example, Marcel Hébert said . . that for simple minds the luminous superiority of the union of the divine with human nature in Jesus Christ was symbolised by the idea of the Virgin Birth, he obviously meant that he could see the truth intended behind the picture of the Nativity presented to the imagination in the Bible story, and the truth he saw he could express more truly than the symbol expressed it by using such phrases as 'the superiority of this particular union of the divine with human nature'. He might still perhaps allow the symbol to occupy his imagination in order to stimulate feeling, but when he wanted to express what he believed to be the real truth he could do so in the phrase given. Being able to contemplate both the symbolic picture and the reality behind it, he could compare one with the other and definitely see how the symbol was *only* a symbol, that is, how it was *unlike* the reality.

The other class of symbols are those behind

which we cannot see, such as many ideas we use
to represent the life of God, if, as we are told, they
have only analogical, and not literal, truth. When
we speak of the love of God or the will of God, we
know that we are speaking of something different
from any love or any will we can know in men,
and the ideas 'love of God', 'will of God', may in
that sense be regarded as an element in the life of
man taken to symbolise something unimaginable
in the life of God. We cannot see behind the
symbol: we cannot have any discernment of the
reality better and truer than the symbolical idea,
and we cannot compare the symbol with the reality as it is more truly apprehended and see how
they differ. The symbol is the nearest we can get
to the Reality.*

2   In earlier chapters we have pressed this question: How may we discover the proper or true meaning of things which are said about God by way of
analogy? This question assumes that the things said
about God are said in symbols that can be seen
behind. But it is not clear that the traditional theory
of analogy was meant to be taken in this way. Perhaps it is pointless to ask for the rule by which to
translate analogical statements into other terms
representing more nearly what they really mean.
Perhaps the analogies are themselves the nearest we
can get.

3   That seems to be the intention of certain
defences and extensions of the theory on the basis of
belief in God as responsible for everything. God
made us, it is said. We are his 'creatures'. Everything around us is, originally, his effect. Now a creature must always resemble its creator, in essential
ways. It bears his 'stamp'. For everything it has it
owes to him. And he could not have created it as it

is, had he not 'had it in him' to author such a thing. So what God is must include everything his creatures really are. All creation's perfections must have flourished in the creator first – though perhaps in a more outstanding way.

4   This argument rests on a basic principle of thought, that is on one which can hardly itself be established or refuted by further argument. Given that one and one make two, one can try to show, to prove by argument, that two and two make four. But it's no good trying to *show* that one and one make two, for there is nothing prior that we could show it from. One is our starting point. It seems equally impossible to *show* that creatures resemble or represent their creators, that a cause must be 'as good as' its effect, that what is responsible for some new thing must be sufficient or adequate to account for it. You either think this or you don't. To encourage you to think it, all I can do is produce persuasive examples, which – if they persuade – will show that you had thought it (i.e. worked on that basis) all along. A teacher (I may urge) must be more knowledgeable than his pupils, for how can he pass on (make in them) knowledge that he has not got? The detective needs to be cleverer than his criminal. Wesley could not make bishops, for he wasn't one.

5   Some of these instances favour the principle 'at least as good', others require 'better than'. But a creator 'equal or superior' to many different creatures in many different ways will be simply superior to each of them singly, as having perfections which not that, but the *other* creatures adumbrate.

6   Every good thing that we have or know, then, existed first of all in God. We have love or understanding only because he first loved or understood. From him 'all fatherhood in heaven and earth is

named'.* God's fatherhood is presumably somewhat *un*like human fatherhood; and it is only
through having a father that we get the idea and so
are able to attribute it to God. But if we are talking
of how things are, and how they got the way they
are, we must say that fatherhood in God comes
first.*

7   It does not come first in our knowledge. We
always have to begin from the things that are nearest to us. Only at a very late stage shall we rise to the
originating principles. Seen from our end, human
fatherhood comes first, and God is called (or miscal-
led) *father* by projection or transference from this.
From our point of view, if fatherhood in God is different then he is called *father* improperly, or by analogy. That is the order in which we get to know these
things. But it is not therefore, and is not in fact, the
order in which they ultimately stand. In the real
order of beings God stands always first.

8   We must therefore distinguish, in theological
terms at least, between what they really mean and
what they mean to us. If our language is inadequate
that is no fault of the things we are failing to describe. Terms applied to God, such as love or even
anger, may well be defective in the meaning they
convey to us, but the object to which they refer –
that which they 'really' mean – is not defective. He
is what he is, and is perfect, irrespective of the predicates by which we try to babble about him.

9   This distinction between the 'mode of signification' and the 'reality signified' comes in very handy
when dealing with awkward statements in a sacred
text. It stands written, for example, that God got
cross with Saul for stopping at genocide, in the case
of the Amalekites, and not destroying all their property as well.* This description is a little difficult to

square with other things said of God in the same compendium, for example, that he loves everyone. The first statement can however be reconciled with the second (or, if you prefer, the second with the first) by saying that it is true of the object signified and defective only in its mode of signification.

10 A plain-speaking man might prefer to say 'false as stated, though it might be true if it said something different'. But plain speaking on religious matters has usually been thought unwise and even impious. In generations which seriously conceived and actually employed the idea of blasphemy a good many consciences may have been relieved by using this dodge: – 'true in what it really means, though with room for improvement in the meaning it conveys to us'.

11 Let us now summarise the revised and extended theory of analogy:- (i) Terms when applied to God mean something different, but their meaning in this application is connected in some intelligible way with what they usually mean; i.e. the religious statements are not meaningless or purely equivocal.

(ii) God as creator must 'have in him' all creation's perfections; e.g. if some creatures are wise then God must be wise too, though not in their way of being wise, but appropriately, i.e. there must be something not unlike wisdom in God, to account for some of his creatures being wise. For lack of any better name we had better apply the term *Wisdom* to this facet of divinity.

12 Putting (i) and (ii) together we may infer that if some statements about God are somehow established we need not worry too much what those statements really mean. They will not mean exactly what they say, yet we cannot say what else they mean, for we have no better words; but we can be sure that

their real meaning – the truth behind them – is entirely satisfactory. The shortcomings in our mode of signifying God's perfections do not detract from their reality; and that reality is so important that it must do some good to try to express it, no matter how defectively. Theology is quite impossible, so theologians' babblings are not a bad attempt, and are deeply significant and more or less invaluable.*

13   Is this theory clear and coherent, when thus extended and revised? If coherent, is it true, or at least acceptable? Before answering, we shall need to say something about the scope or extension of the theory. Is it meant to apply to all religious statements? Or to all *symbolic* statements about God? Or only to some of these? and, if so, to which?

VIII. Is the Theory Subject to Analogy?

SOME say no statements about God can be literally true, as no human concepts can be adequate to the divine. All theological statements, without exception, must be taken as subject to analogy (see II, 4 *ante*).

2   Someone who says that no human concepts can be adequate to the divine claims, in effect, to know quite a lot about divinity; viz., that it is such that all human concepts are *and must be* inadequate to it. And *this* knowledge of divinity can (he assumes) be expressed precisely enough to form the basis of a human argument. Human reasoners can be properly convinced of the conclusion *that no human concepts, etc. etc.* But no argument can be accepted which contains unknown or uncertain terms. So there will have to be one statement, at least, about God which is, and is known to be, literally true; viz., that God is such that all human concepts etc. etc. Which brings us round again, but to another starting point.

3   Like many abstract or 'philosophical' arguments about whole departments of knowledge or experience, this one if taken seriously will undermine itself. That is not to say the conclusion is false, but only that its truth, if it is true, cannot possibly be established by this line of argument.

4   To avoid these logical puzzles it is often held, that some statements *about* God are literally true and can be known to us: we can prove that there must be

a God, One who does not just happen to exist and who is perfect and infinite in every way. This knowledge of ours about God is not subject to analogy; and it is from this literal knowledge that we can show our own incapacity to comprehend God's real, inner, personal nature, and thence that all human statements describing that nature must fail to describe it, if taken literally. Thus a proof of God's existence and infinity, expressed in non-analogical terms, shows (without undermining itself) that every description of God's nature must be taken as subject to analogy.†

5 Can direct descriptions of God be clearly marked off, as this apology requires, from indirect statements 'about' him? The latter are mostly relational, and ultimately negative. For instance, if we say that God is immaterial we are not so much describing him as saying something 'about' him, stating his relation of dissimilarity to other things more familiar to us. It is not incoherent to say that the unknown subject of theological predicates, the mysterious One whom we call perfect and infinite and omniscient, has no weight and occupies no space.

6 The flaw in the distinction, thus drawn, lies in its other half. Are there then some predicates which are *not* relational and do not involve comparison? It is difficult to think of one, in theology. If there are no 'direct descriptions' at all, in the sense required, then saying there are no direct descriptions of God is not saying very much. And if the proposed distinction between direct and indirect descriptions turns out to be undrawable we can hardly use it to separate safely off those literal (but indirect) statements about God which we need in order to establish the theory of anal-

ogy as applying to all the *rest* of theology.
7 Another way out of this impasse would be to restrict the conclusion, that no statements about God
can be literally true, so that it no longer undermines
itself. Certainly overstatement seems second nature
to piety. Some people feel that if a thesis says something nice about God and rude about us that is in
itself, and in the absence of evidence, a good reason
for propounding it. When pressed for reasons these
folk grant readily that the thesis may not be actually
true. That, they imply, would be aiming too high.
But it was, they claim, appropriate. It put us in our
proper place. So it should be said again, with
emphasis.
8 This peculiar duty (of telling purple lies) can
perhaps be left to those who like to mortify their
intellects. Let us look for the truth which their over-
statements overstate. It may be, in the present case,
that no statements about God can be *known to be* literally true, because no human concepts can be *shown
to be* adequate to the divine. This would make it possible to say that all of theology may be subject to
analogy, without undermining anything (except the
dogmatism that accompanies so much theology).
9 The force of this little amendment 'known to be'
may perhaps become clearer if we adduce a parallel
from a more cultivated corner of philosophy.
Immanuel Kant made his name by suggesting that
the constant and invariable features of human experience – timing, spatial relationship, number,
size, causality – might really be part of the
observer's way of seeing things. For if we are so
made as naturally to notice things one after another,
then naturally all that we notice will appear to us as
temporal. If in seeing things we automatically relate
them to one another as 'on top' or 'alongside' or

'behind' etc., then all that we see is bound to seem to us to be 'in space'. And so on. Now, said Kant, Time and Space being really our contribution to the scene, they really belong only to things-as-they-appear-to-us. The Reality that lies behind appearances must properly be non-spatial and a-temporal*. At this point (and this is the point of the comparison for us) Kant went beyond his brief. The universality and felt necessity of timing and spacing in human experience does not show that we do contribute Time and Space, but only that we *may*. Supposing we do. Supposing our way of knowing and perceiving things were in fact such as to cause a-temporal and non-spatial things to appear to us as timed and spaced, that still would not *prove* the ultimate Reality behind the whole façade to be non-spatial and a-temporal, but would only open this up as a (mind-boggling) *possibility*. Kant suggests that maybe *we* are all the time timing things and spacing them out everywhere. This suggestion has not been disproved. All that it shows is that statements of temporal and spatial relationships cannot be *known to be* true of ultimate Reality.

10   With this lantern in our hands let us look again in the dark corners of theology. God being (what we falteringly call) perfect and infinite and beyond our ken in every way etc. etc., no human concepts can be shown to be adequate for describing the divine, so nothing (else) that we say about him can be known to be literally true. The whole of theology (including this bit) *may be* subject to analogy.

11   This argument is in the happy position that it may not undermine itself. For on this view God may after all be precisely what some of our human adjectives describe. And though we cannot say for certain which of the terms we apply to God are properly

and literally true of him, these privileged predicates may – for all we could possibly know to the contrary – include those employed in setting up the theory of analogy. If this conclusion makes people feel uncomfortable, let us offer the thought that it is humbler not to be so jolly sure that we are ignorant.

12 An argument that may hold good sometimes though we can't say when, is no earthly use as an argument, for it could never license us to rely on the conclusion because of our confidence in the premisses. If this argument, the only one available, is no earthly use, then there is no prospect of establishing the theory of analogy by means of argument.

13 The possibility that some things we say about God may, unbeknownst to us, be literally true does not however prevent us from stating the theory of analogy in a universal form. For the exceptions can be brought under the rule as cases of zero interpretation. The rule says that everything said about God is to be taken in a sense appropriate to his infinite perfection. We cannot so understand it, where the concept used is in fact inappropriate; for if we could 'understand' or interpret a partly inappropriate concept in a more appropriate way, and express this understanding in proper terms, then we would drop that first concept and use this other which we now see to be more appropriate. Why talk of phlogiston when the term 'oxidation' has been shown to be more suitable? But suppose some other beings, e.g. angels, have a proper understanding of that Reality which we riddlingly refer to in our theology. Then they will see that in the (presumably) exceptional cases where our concept is in fact appropriate to its object, that concept is as the rule says being 'appropriately understood', and so need not be made an exception to our theory of analogy.

14   In this catholic form the theory states that all things said about God are to be understood (if only it were possible) appropriately, and that some at least will really mean something different. Restricting ourselves in thought to these, whichever they may be, let us ask if all such symbols are irreducible. Does analogy apply, in a practical way, only to symbols that we cannot see behind?

IX. Irreducibles

ON THE extended theory of analogy some things said about God 'are true in what they really mean but leave room for improvement in the meaning they convey to us'. But is there always room for improvement in what these predicates convey *to us*? No, says Bevan, there are some symbols that we cannot hope to see behind (VII. 1, *ante*) They may indeed need improving in the meaning they convey, but no such improvement is going to come our way.

2   Take *fatherhood in God*, for example. Can the matter here referred to be put into other, clearer terms? Or is *father* already the nearest that we can get to it? If it is, then we must rest content with this image in practice, though admitting that in theory it is 'subject to analogy'. All we can do to bring out its inevitable inadequacy is to assert along with it other equally irreducible images like *ruler* and *judge*, which if they were taken literally would be inconsistent in some ways with the literal meaning conveyed by *father* when applied to God.

3   There seems to be no way of deciding in advance whether a symbol is irreducible. For no-one can now say for certain whether or not someone will at some future date improve on *father* and find a better way of saying what that was intended to convey. But we can discover if someone now thinks he sees a better way, simply by asking if the proffered symbol ('A') is meant to be taken seriously. If he says No, and

offers another one ('X') in place of it, we may take him to think that X expresses better what A was meant to say. If he hesitates, and then says that of course all our language is subject to the limitations of humanity, we may take him to think that A is the nearest *he* can get to the heart of the matter. So we can in practice divide symbols into those which their users do, and those they do not, claim to see behind.

4   The theory of analogy can be applied to symbols of both varieties. Its main theoretical interest however is in application to the latter sort, the symbols which the user makes no claim to see behind but regards as practically ultimate. For with symbols which the user does claim to see behind, the work of the theory of analogy is in a sense already done.

5   Let us look at an instance of a religious symbol which the user claims to see behind, and consider the effect on it of the theory of analogy. Suppose someone says God did something 'with a mighty hand and stretched out arm'. That seems a very human way of putting it. Presumably we are not meant to take it literally. And the speaker agrees. Questions about thumbs and biceps are quite out of place. What he meant (he says) was that God's action on that occasion was related to his other actions in the way that a human action done 'with a mighty hand and stretched out arm' is related to other human actions. But that seemed a mouthful to say; so he said that God did it in a (divinely) strong-arm sort of way. Which could perhaps be better expressed by saying that in that action or event the power of God was very evident. And why is that a better way of putting it? Well, it does not so obviously call for further qualification and interpretation. Almost everyone

knows that God hasn't really got an arm!†
6   I am not suggesting that we can decide by simple
inspection that 'in evident exercise of the divine
power' or, for short, 'miraculously', is a better way
to speak of God than 'with a mighty hand and
stretched-out arm'. This goes back to the more general question of how we decide to regard some statements about God as true or, at least, acceptable.
Some will hope to establish 'that God is A' by means
of argument. In that case the argument itself should
show if X would be a better thing to say. Some rely
on their own personal and 'innermost' convictions to
decide if God is A. They should be able to enquire
within to see if God is (really) X. Some trust the
convictions of others more than their own, and will
accept anything that Moses was sure of, or it may be
Mahomet, or Joseph Smith. But in whatever way
one supposes that 'God is A' is to be established, one
should be able in that same way to decide if 'God is
X' is a better thing to say.
7   Now if we can in some agreeable way decide that
a given translation 'works', i.e. that some X says the
same as A was meant to say, and says it better, i.e.
less inappropriately, then we shall forthwith lose interest in A and concentrate on X. The theory of
analogy will have done its work (on A), once we
show that symbol X is available and is more appropriate. And as we now have both concepts in hand,
A and X, we can if we wish compare them directly.
We no longer need a general theory to sketch out
their possible relationship. The question now is, can
X in its turn be improved on, and reduced to Y?
8   Supposing it can, and supposing that Y is then
reduced to Z. . . . Presumably this process of reduction and replacement will come to an end at some
point. There must – if the whole chain of symbolic

equivalence is not to be suspended in thin air – be some N which is absolutely the best discoverable human way of putting A (and X, and Y, and Z. . . .). N cannot, as far as we can see, be improved on or reduced or any further qualified. So N, at least, is a symbol that we do not claim to see behind. And once we have N we lose interest in Z and Y and X and A. What we now want to know is how we are to understand our final symbol, N. It is with such irreducible symbols that the theory of analogy is finally and fundamentally and importantly concerned.

9   Does it follow that whatever is said about God in the clearest conceivable way must be thought of as subject to analogy? Yes, if that clearest way is still symbolic. But it might not be. For in some contexts the ultimate and irreducible translation is not symbolic but precise. Take for instance the slightly purple Rhodesian phrase 'kith and kin'. This might be translated, in a given case, by 'second cousin once removed'. This needs no further translation. It is 'N'. But it also means exactly what it says. It is not a symbol, in our present sense. So it is not a symbol-which-we-cannot-just-now-see-behind.

10   Some say that no human statements about God can be literally true. If this is true (quite literally) then in every religious statement the ultimate and irreducible N will still be a symbol, and so will be subject to analogy, i.e. its usual meaning will be partly inappropriate, though as it is also irreducible we cannot say in what way or part it is inappropriate. I have argued earlier (VIII. *ante*) that we cannot be sure that *all* human statements about God are positively inappropriate, though any one of them may be, for all we would know to the contrary; and that to state the deficiencies of human theology so strongly is actually to claim to know a lot about

divinity, a claim which undercuts itself. It is better to say that as any such statement may be inappropriate all should be *taken as* subject to analogy (VIII. 13,14, *ante*).

11   The scope of the theory may now be summarised:

    (i) No statement about God can be known to be literally true, though some may be so in fact.

    (ii) Some symbolic statements about God can be replaced by other statements which are less obviously inappropriate. The statements replaced may then be discarded.

    (iii) When all such replacement is finished the remaining statements are either literal or symbolic.

    (iv) We cannot tell which, if any, of them are literal.

    (v) The symbolic statements remaining when all replacement is finished contain symbols that we cannot just now see behind; i.e. we know that they don't really mean quite what they say (they are symbolic) yet we can't say quite what they do mean (we can't see behind them). Such statements may best be made 'subject to analogy', i.e. with the constant qualification that the meaning they convey to us is inadequate to the subject they are intended to describe.

12   Three questions remain:

    (i) Is the theory of analogy (as amended and now limited in scope) coherent?

    (ii) Is it acceptable, as applied to irreducibles?

    (iii) If accepted, what are its consequences for

x. Being Told the Right Thing to Say

TAKE first the thesis that God must resemble his creatures sufficiently to account for them. This rests on a principle which cannot be proved or even stated satisfactorily, but which we would all appeal to in certain cases, the principle that a cause must be at least 'as good' as its effect. (VII. 4, *ante*). Lacking wider or more fundamental principles by which to judge this one, the best we can do is think of instances to which we would readily apply it and then of others where it seems less plausible.

2 In matters of knowledge and intelligence no one, we presume, can pass on what he has not got. He must be 'up to it', In a chain of command higher rank goes with greater authority; all orders come from 'higher up'. It takes one noble already to confer nobility. In the case of holy orders (on the pipeline view) sacredness and separateness have to be duly received from an authentic source before they can be validly conferred.

3 On the other hand, the beauty of a face or a landscape may inspire a painter to create one yet more beautiful. Then perhaps we should say that the extra (at least) is 'all his own work'. Again, a chance collocation of atoms may exhibit a geometrical pattern – at least to a perceiver who notices such things. Surface peculiarities of objects, at the molecular level, act differentially on different

wavelengths of light, causing us to see colours which surpass a mere wiggle-frequency. Perhaps a random assemblage of proteins once threw up a reproducing molecule and so gave rise to life; after which genetic variation and re-combination occasioned the whole grand sad story of evolution up or down to man.

4   In each of these latter instances some will insist on an extra and external cause to account, to their satisfaction, for that part of the effect which seems unlike and beyond the superficial worldly cause. Others see this as myth-making, and propose to do without the principle (and the explanation too). Their discarding of the principle can be held to show that it is not indispensable. So we may conclude that only those with an innate theistic tendency, evidenced by a general acceptance of this principle of causal 'adaequation' or satisfactoriness (for instance, Anselm, Leibniz and Descartes) will insist that God must resemble his creatures enough in order properly to account for them.

5   How much resemblance is enough? Not having tried making worlds, we cannot say.† But we feel there must be some. So if we ascribe to the Maker some positive and good characteristic found in the world we cannot be entirely wrong.

6   This line of enquiry looks at first as though it might show us what God is actually like, as follows: From the order in created things we first argue that they must have been made for a purpose, then that their maker must have been other-worldly and divine, and finally that He who made this world one and good and great and beautiful must himself be great and good and one and beautiful and true. This argument is apparently about how things actually are, not about how we can come to know and speak

of them; it is an essay in metaphysics, not an extension to the theory of analogy.

7   Such an essay would be unnervingly catholic in its results, for it applies equally to all of God's effects. He is responsible for tigers and liver flukes and leukaemia just as much as for lambs and sunsets and fertility. This point is not much stressed in the language of Christian devotion. For example the children's hymn 'All things bright and beautiful' lists flowers, birds, purple-headed mountains (i.e. in sunshine in August), river, sunset, summer sun, ripe fruits, tall trees, meadows and 'The rushes by the water We gather every day'; all things most people would call bright or beautiful or at least pleasant and desirable. The hymn then concludes 'How great is God Almighty Who has made all things well' though the conclusion really licensed by the earlier verses would be 'some things'. If the argument from effect to sufficiently similar cause is valid, then the qualities found in tigers and liver flukes and leukaemia must also have their (supreme and perfected) analogues in God, and if we called God vital and ruthless, destructive and insidious we would not be further out than if we stuck to the more usual adjectives. This conclusion is embraced by Hindu theologians, who say that God has three aspects, Creator, Sustainer and Destroyer, and that the destructive aspect, which is popularly called Kali and Durga and somewhat gruesomely portrayed, may just as well be worshipped as the other two; a rather heroic 'honesty to God', but at least consistent and impartial in its application of the Sufficient-cause argument.

8   When we turn from the positive content of the various conclusions to the invariable accompanying qualification, things look rather different. The

argument from creation allows us to say almost anything about God, but we always add that no one can tell how far what we have said is right. This vagueness renders the argument nearly useless as a way of finding out about Reality, but makes it very handy as an extension to our theory of analogy. Its practical effect is more linguistic than metaphysical.

9   Suppose there were available some officially authorised remarks about divinity: that God is loving and wise and powerful. Suppose also that we feel the force of the theist's argument from infinity, and conclude that no human concepts (such as *powerful, loving,* or *wise*) can be adequate to the divine. We look like becoming agnostics. But then we are reassured. For the love and the wisdom and power that we come across in God's creatures must somehow have their source 'in him'. He must possess these qualities in some way, or he could not be responsible for them. So we are not wrong, after all, in calling God loving, wise and powerful, for he must have some characteristics actually beyond our present ken but in some definite way analogous to these. And if these particular qualities are officially authorised for ascription to divinity, ascribing them may be the nearest we can get to saying what he is.

10   The thesis that God as creator must resemble his creatures does not enable us to say any more surely or sufficiently what he is really like. But it does guarantee a meaning, of sorts, to the things we already want to say. This guarantee extends, of course, to anything anyone may want to say. Babbling with deep significance is not a Christian monopoly.

11   This support – if we can call it that – may do for the language of devotion, but it really 'does for' any argumentative theology. Before, however, we set out

its disastrous effects on reasoning let us look once again at the apologist's phrase 'true of what is meant but inadequate in the meaning it conveys to us'.

12   To say that the 'thing signified' (*res significata*) is true seems at first a simple confusion, for things or objects or entities cannot properly be called either true or false; only statements can. But *res* also means 'matter' or 'affair'. This yields 'the matter under description is truly so but the description given is inadequate'. Which is like saying 'what I said was wrong but what I should have said was right'; a pleasant way of admitting that my statement was inaccurate.

13   There is no salvaging this thesis so long as we take 'what I should have said' as expressible more properly. If it could be said better, my job is to find out how. Until I do, apologies are out of place. But apologies are all right if it can't be said better; if it is said in symbols that we cannot see behind.

14   If we admit that there are or could be 'truths which we are trying, and failing to express' then these can be the 'matter signified'. The thesis now says 'what I am trying to express is true, though I know I haven't managed to express it yet, and quite likely never will, for I don't know what it is'. As a footnote to a prayer that shows a suitable humility. As a preface to dogmatic ('teaching') theology it is completely agnostic in effect. If an author says on page one that what follows is certainly wrong, and that something else – though no one knows what – is right, only connoisseurs of error will persevere to page two.

15   The thesis that God must resemble his creatures, possessing (though in another form) all the perfections that he put in them, is descriptively

empty. It does not enable us to say more faithfully what God is like. Indeed, it empties all present descriptions of the specific meanings that they seemed to have. In exchange, it offers a vague and general assurance that the things we say about God may not totally mislead. And if those things have come in a package labelled 'guaranteed' it encourages us to take them on trust, confident that there is a Reality to which they are inadequate.

16   Trusting souls will readily believe that God would have given them quite the best symbols anywhere available; so that their theology, though false, is the nearest any human thought can come to Truth. If there are several different theologies on offer these trusting souls – if consistent – would either have to restrict such a claim to one of them or else say that, for all they know, the alternative theologies may not be really different.

17   There are in fact many seemingly different theologies on the market. Even within official Christianity there are five or six. To choose between them in the dark, i.e. without reference to their unintelligible contents, one would need some external light by which to check the handwriting on the label saying 'guaranteed'. In the absence of such an extrinsic distinction a preference for one of them as *really* guaranteed may be called (according to one's standpoint) a leap of faith, a basic presupposition, a dogma, or just bigoted.

18   Alternatively, one may refuse to choose between competing theologies, saying that we know they must really say the same. If one really meant this, one had better stop listening to all of them, for what each seems to be saying must in most cases be different from what all really mean. In practice, people who say this usually stick with the theology

they started with, saying that one has to be brought up to it to understand it properly: an uncomforting thought for converts. In practice, then, this 'refusal to choose' turns out to be a slightly politer form of the 'leap of faith' (or, bigotry).

19   If there are several different theologies on offer, any or all of which could have come from God, and none of them properly intelligible (i.e. meaning what it says), then the real choice is between, at some point, refusing to think, and ceasing to suppose that God must have given us the best symbols anywhere available† Why should he? Perhaps he means us to go out and look for them.

20   The extended theory of analogy, I conclude, is coherent, though it is much more agnostic than has been usually supposed. It remains to ask if there are, or could be, good reasons for accepting the theory; and, if so, what effect it will have upon theology.

4. Effect of the Theory on Theology

xi. Not Proven

THE ONLY known reason for accepting the theory of analogy is that as God is infinite no human concepts can be adequate to him (IV. 4, *ante*). This argument involves some dubious assumptions: that whatever is finite is to that extent also imperfect, and that ideas adequate to their objects must also somehow be commensurate with them. But those who propound this argument, and those to whom they propound it, do not need to be convinced. They already hold, as a matter of piety and almost of morality, that terms which are true of God cannot be true in their ordinary sense.

2   If this argument were somehow refurbished, the holes stopped up and the principles of inference made more plausible, the question would still arise whether the argument is available to us. For if its conclusion is correct we can call God creator and infinite only by analogy, and we cannot tell how appropriate these appellations are to him. But in that case we cannot estimate the strength of the argument *from* his infinity and creative work *to* the inadequacy of these and all other human terms as applied to him. If we accept the conclusion we make the argument dubious once again.

3   Oddly enough the converse also holds. If we reject the conclusion and assert that terms applied to God can and should be taken literally, we thereby reinstate the argument, which now (if valid) proves

that theological terms are to be taken as subject to analogy. Each party to this semantic dispute can rejoice at the other's discomfiture in the moment of his seeming victory.

4   The pattern of this little puzzle is nowadays familiar. It is parallel to that of the Cretan who said 'all Cretans are liars' which, if true, is thereby shown to be false; and if false, true. Some logicians have tried to banish such puzzles by prohibiting all self-reference, though it is hard to see why only Cretans should be forbidden to make statements about Cretans as a class. Until an agreed solution emerges we can only note that our paradox is similar in form to these and hope (as no one knows the answer) that it isn't very serious.

5   Some exponents avoid this knot by claiming certain exceptions to the theory: creation and infinity are to be taken literally while setting up the theory (VIII. 4, *ante*). But unless we show that these epithets remain exceptions this is mere sleight-of-hand. Establishing a conclusion by means of premises which then have to be denied or doubted is *not* like climbing a wall and then throwing the ladder away while standing on the wall.* It is more like constructing a scaffold from several interlocking poles and then climbing up it to pull out one on which the whole edifice depends.

6   If the argument required to establish the theory of analogy is so shaky and ambiguous, can we do without the argument? Yes, if we believe the conclusion anyhow. Those already convinced that statements about God are all more or less inappropriate and imprecise will be interested in any theory which offers to explain and assess and, perhaps, remedy this imprecision and inadequacy. And one religious-language-user may commend such a theory to

another in the way one commends an interpretation of a poem or a symphony, by saying that when taken this way it all suddenly fits in. It is when people wish to argue their way from one theological proposition to another that the difficulties begin.

7   Anyone engaged in arguing is trying to show someone else that he must accept proposition C if he already accepts propositions A and B. Now the rules of argument have been worked out only for cases where A and B and C mean exactly what they say. If either party holds that A and B, or C, mean something different, they will need to settle this point before proceeding to the argument. And here 'settling the point' means displaying just what meanings are after all to be given to A and B and C. Until this is done no one can really 'follow' the argument. One cannot tell whether A and B (as interpreted) support C (as interpreted) unless he knows, or can work out, what element of interpretation is involved.

8   Theologians, then, need to establish their theory of analogy before they start on their theology. And the theory they establish had better be 'gnostic' in effect, i.e. had better tell us how to work out what their statements really mean, otherwise all their arguments will become void for uncertainty. But we have shown that, if properly thought through, the theory of analogy must be agnostic in effect. The result must be to abolish serious argumentative theology.

9   Of the three questions posed earlier (VII. 13, ante) two have now been answered and a start made on answering the third:

(i) Is the extended theory of analogy coherent? Yes, as a statement of our ignorance of the Reality adumbrated by symbols which we cannot see behind. (As an assurance that theologians do know what they are talking about though it's a bit too deep to explain to a layman, the theory is just eyewash, like house agent's guff).

(ii) Is the theory acceptable? (a) Can it be established by means of argument? No. The argument advanced in its support is too shaky to support anything. Moreover the theory if established by means of any argument would debilitate some terms essential to that argument. But denying the theory tends, similarly, to re-establish it. (b) Is the theory acceptable without the argument? Yes. If we agree with the conclusion it seems legitimate, in these circumstances, to consider the theory and forget about the argument.

(iii) What sort of effect does the theory have upon theology? Disastrous. For the theory says that the meanings of terms are uncertain and indeed unknowable by us if the terms are applied by us to God. We are therefore unable to assess the strength of any argument which turns upon those terms. All theological argument is therefore void for uncertainty.

10   Before exploring further (in chapter XIII) this 'agnostic' effect of the theory of analogy, it may be as well to distinguish arguments involving terms subject to analogy (that includes all theological, most psychological and perhaps some cosmological and electrical arguments) from the more familiar 'arguments by analogy'. We must also show how analogy, in this sense, is related to allegory, simile and metaphor.

XII. Arguing by Metaphor

Metaphor, according to the *Concise Oxford Dictionary*, is the 'application of name or descriptive term to an object to which it is not literally applicable (e.g. a *glaring* error)' for an error does not really have eyes with which to stare us in the face. Thus defined, *metaphor* is a generic term covering any and every non-literal use of words. It may be better to restrict it to words and phrases brought into sentences on other topics, i.e. where the sentence as a whole is intended literally and only this word or phrase has to be taken suggestively, as indicating an instructive comparison. Consider 'It was a glaring error to call an election at that time'. This sentence is about *calling an election then*: which, it says, was a mistake, and one so obvious that it seems to 'stare you in the face'. Only this last, descriptive element is to be taken non-literally.

2 Almost all words are metaphorical, if we compare their present meaning with what they originally must have meant. *Metaphor*, for instance, meant something carried over or transferred; *compare* is from a Latin word whose parts mean 'equal together', *present* is from one meaning 'at hand, in attendance'; and so we could go on. This universality of metaphor is good to remember when some Epicurus suggests clearing up the muddles of philosophy simply by using every word in its plain and original sense. But for our present purposes it is

irrelevant. The ordinary, literal meaning of a word is not what it once meant long ago but what it means to people now. It is using a term in a context foreign to its *current* meaning that constitutes a metaphor.

3   *Simile* (again in COD) is 'the introduction . . . of an object or scene or action with which the one in hand is professedly compared'. It is an extended metaphor, a comparison worked out at sentence length. Moreover the reader is told, by the little word *as*, that the writer is attempting to describe one subject by bringing in another for comparison.

4   Both metaphor and simile are ostensibly for illustration, explaining some A by reference to some other, B, that is similar but more familiar; but both are in practice used mainly for effect. A metaphor should be lively or striking; which it will be if B is as dissimilar as possible, in other ways, to A, thus making them unlikely objects for comparison. Take, for instance, a piece of Polonius from the Wayside Pulpit:

Worry, like a rocking chair, gives you something to do but gets you nowhere.

This points a resemblance in one aspect alone between worry and rocking chairs. In all other ways the two are so dissimilar that comparing them at all seems quite remarkable. If this oddity induces us to reflect on the nature and effects of worry for a week, or a day, or just for a bit of that bus journey, the metaphor will have achieved its desired effect.

5   *Allegory* is defined as 'narrative description of a subject under guise of another suggestively similar'. It usually contains a story, not just one action or a static scene. It is not always signalled by a special word. To make an allegory we need two items or

sequences showing numerous similarities; and one
of the main functions of the comparison is to suggest
further instructive or amusing points of comparison.
In an allegory this suggestion is usually for wit or
amusement or, sometimes, for ambiguity and con-
cealment. Either way, the effect is spoilt if we spell
all the correspondence out. In an analogy, however,
the comparison is for enlightenment, of both parties,
and the main benefit comes from spelling it out, for
even the person proposing it may not yet have
worked out the significance of all the corre-
spondences.
6   *Analogy* was a term of mathematics first, meaning ratio or proportion. It was later extended to
cover any similarity or comparison, especially a
comparison of relationships. A relationship is an
abstract thing not easily grasped or defined except
by stating the related terms. If one of these needs
explaining, the simplest way is by appeal to a
similar relation between terms more familiar. Thus
the relation between a manuscript and one of its re-
moter copies may be brought vividly to mind by borrowing terms from the parallel relationship of
human ancestry, like *brother* and *grandfather*. Incomplete analogies of this sort can be used in examina-
tions to test comprehension of relative terms without
defining them, thus:-

umpire is to cricketer as —— is to footballer
—— is to able seaman as sergeant is to private

Not that these puzzles are always unambiguous, for
one term may stand in several relationships. We
might say

grandfather is to father as father is to son   (i.e.
male parent of)

but we could also say

   . . . as guardian to ward   (legally responsible)

and we could compare this with 'uncle to nephew', 'husband to wife', 'master to servant' (i.e. just corre- latives).

7   The first purpose of these verbal diagrams is to state relationships. But they are also suggestive, like allegory, of further comparisons. If a guardian is (legally) like a father to his ward, should he also act like one, being fatherly in ways the law cannot re- quire or impute? There is, it seems, a natural ten- dency to move from the discovery of one similarity between two items to the expectation of further simi- larities, a tendency strengthened by every fresh dis- covery, and called by logicians 'argument by analogy'. Let us take a well-known instance to watch this tendency at work.

8   Plato in his *Republic* compares the state with the individual. Three elements go to make up the body politic: rulers, police, and working class. Three similar elements, similarly related, can (he says) be made out in the psychology of the individual: reason, which rules; spirit or indignation, which enforces the rulings of reason, and the unruly mob of wants or desires.* This elaborate comparison is offered as an aid in discovering what constitutes 'justice' or 'right' or 'fairness' in the individual. It also unites and illustrates the two main functions of analogy already discussed:

   (i) It offers a verbal diagram of a complex rela- tionship,
  (ii) Noting certain admitted similarities between the two items compared, it encourages us to search for further similarities.

9   The phrase 'argument by analogy' suggests that
analogies perform a third function, that of showing a
certain conclusion as supported by the acceptance of
certain premisses. In an argument by analogy
(according to the logic-books), two items A and B
being found to share two features X and Y, this is
taken as a reason for believing that, if A also has feature Z, B will (probably) have it too. In the present
instance Plato, if he is arguing by analogy, will
invite us to believe that individual, like political, justice consists in mutual non-interference between the
three parts or elements involved, on the ground that
the soul or individual, like the state, is made up of
three parts, and that the wisdom of each resides in
its ruling part.

10   It does not take a logician long to show that
such reasoning (like the supposed 'argument by
induction' to which it is formally parallel) is quite
without probative force; that B's possession of Z
cannot be proved from A possessing it and their
both possessing X and Y. Some logicians conclude,
inconsequentially, that B's having Z must therefore
be 'made probable' by those grounds, though they
do not say how probable, nor can they explain
satisfactorily what it means to say that a certain
argument makes its conclusion probable.

11   In this doubtful situation we owe it to Plato to
ask if he really argues in this way. The analogy is
first suggested in book II:

> Now, as we are not remarkably clever, I will
> make a suggestion as to how we should proceed.
> Imagine a rather short-sighted person told to
> read an inscription in small letters from some
> way off. He would think it a godsend if someone
> pointed out that the same inscription was written

up elsewhere on a bigger scale, so that he could first read the larger characters and then make out whether the smaller ones were the same.*

12   That last clause means that the analogy is not put forward as an argument, i.e. a reason for accepting the conclusion on the basis of the premises alone, but as a suggestion for further investigation. Does Plato stick to this? The comparison between state and individual is first worked out in detail, then the (four traditional) virtues defined as they occur in the state. Plato's Socrates goes on:

> We must not be too positive yet, said I. If we find that this same quality when it exists in the individual can equally be identified with justice, then we can at once give our assent; there will be no more to be said; otherwise, we shall have to look further. For the moment, we had better finish the enquiry which we began with the idea that it would be easier to make out the nature of justice in the individual if we first tried to study it in something on a larger scale. That larger thing we took to be a state, and so we set about constructing the best one we could, being sure of finding justice in a state that was good. The discovery we made there must now be applied to the individual. If it is confirmed, all will be well; but if we find that justice in the individual is something different, we must go back to the state and test our new result. Perhaps if we brought the two cases into contact like flint and steel, we might strike out between them the spark of justice, and in its light confirm the conception in our own minds.

He then produces independent grounds for distinguishing three functions or 'parts' in the individual. And it looks as though he will use the analogy only for 'suggestive' purposes. But he continues:

> We are fairly agreed that the same three elements exist alike in the state and in the individual soul. – That is so. – Does it not follow at once that state and individual will be wise or brave by virtue of the same element in each and in the same way? Both will possess in the same manner any quality that makes for excellence. – That must be true. – Then it applies to justice: we shall conclude that a man is just in the same way that a state was just. And we have surely not forgotten that justice in the state meant that each of the three orders in it was doing its own proper work. So we may henceforth bear in mind that each of us likewise will be a just person, fulfilling his proper function, only if the several parts of our nature fulfil theirs.*

13   It looks as though he has fallen back, in the end, on using the analogy as itself an argument. But on Platonic assumptions the analysis of the individual soul into three functions has itself provided sufficient for us to construct an independent argument. For, given that

(i) justice is an excellence

(ii) an excellence of anything must consist in the peculiar constitution of that thing, i.e. either of the excellence of some of its parts or in their mutual relationships

(iii) justice in the state consists in a certain relationship between its parts

(iv) the individual is constituted of similar parts
        similarly related,

then – unless *justice* is to be quite ambiguous and
equivocal – it follows directly that justice must be
similarly defined in the individual.

14   Plato can be defended, then, against the charge
of 'arguing by analogy' at this point; though the
defender has to admit that Plato's Socrates has not
on this occasion quite spelt out the argument. To
return now to our main question: Can analogies
properly function as arguments? We may divide this
into two distinct queries: i. Is it a popular and natural form of inference? ii. Can it ever by a valid one?

15   It is popular, and presumably persuasive. One
who says 'If you don't like the Church's rules you'd
better leave' is appealing to the analogy, such as it
is, between the Church and a voluntary society for
yachting or canasta or philately. One who says 'I
am the real vine, and my father is the gardener' is
comparing disciples to branches, pruning to disci-
pline, and inferring that disciples 'die' if 'cut off'
from their 'source of life'.

16   Such arguments are invalid. But it would be
time ill spent to explore the precise form and degree
of invalidity of them *as arguments*, for that is not their
main function, and only the foolish or unwary
repose faith in their conclusions solely on the basis
of their premises. Taken as suggestions, however,
they are quite instructive. It is useful to look and see
if the Church is a club, or not, and to consider
whether a disciple must always 'follow my leader',
for ever *in statu pupillari*, or whether his master may
be thought to want him to grow up and think things
out for himself.

17   The suggestion an analogy conveys may be
implicit or explicit. An explicit suggestion is often

set out inferentially, with a 'therefore' or a 'so':

(A) Nickel is hard and shiny and ductile, like copper and lead and zinc, so it may also, like them, conduct electricity.

An implicit suggestion is one conveyed by the deliberate 'borrowing' of a descriptive term proper to another field:

(B) electric force is said to 'flow' in a 'current' (as its passage has some properties resembling those of a flow of water)

This metaphor or conceptual 'model' may suggest to us further testable properties or relationships of electric force, for instance those called (again by implicit analogy) 'resistance'.*

18   In both implicit and explicit analogies the main function of the analogy is to suggest further possible similarities, and the sensible thing to do next is check up on these suggestions, to see if 'the analogy holds' in those respects. But in some cases we are not at present in a position to check up. Our faith in the suggestion made can therefore only repose on the analogy itself. For instance:

(X) Mercury is round like the earth, and has an atmosphere, and its surface temperature (judging by its distance from the sun) may well be below 100°C, so it may, like the earth, support some form of life.

19   A scientist who thinks this analogy 'sound' will keep its conclusion in mind as a possibility in case he should ever come across ways of checking up on it. To that limited extent he could be said to rely on the analogy. Other people may be inclined to dispense with the check-up and accept the conclusion

as somehow established by the 'argument'. But then some people will accept the conclusion of a syllogism simply because the premisses are true. Such actions do not merit extended consideration in a logic-book.

20   We could however use this sort of argument-by-analogy (X) as third term in a proportion (or 'analogy'!) relating theological analogy (Y) to the explicit (A) and implicit (B) analogies used in other spheres:

$$A : B \quad :: \quad X : Y$$

A and X are set out in propositions. Both are suggestions, but in the case of X we cannot see how to check up on it, and we may be inclined to repose some faith in its conclusion even in the absence of evidence, and simply on the strength of the analogy. Y and B are single-term analogies, or conceptual 'models'. Y, like B, suggests various possible descriptions or similarities, but in the case of Y there is no way to verify independently which of these are appropriate in fact, or how appropriate. So we use Y to generate descriptive terms, adding *sotto voce* 'just in so far, of course, as these may be in fact appropriate'.

21   That saving clause (if remembered) makes this a pretty safe policy; for it is an almost infallible way of being right on the whole, to admit cheerfully that on any given detail you may well be wrong. And if this is the best that we can do, as it seems to be, in theology, then perhaps we had better grin and carry on; though some stern people would say it is better not to carry on. It is wrong, they say, to believe anything in the absence of compelling evidence,† or to repose any faith in untestable analogies; and they would probably think it equally wrong to employ

terms which might in the end turn out to be inappropriate.

22   A reasonable man, says Locke, always proportions his assent to the evidence. One may try, similarly, to proportion one's faith to the strength of an
analogy. That is not to say we can measure such
'strength' objectively, but we do regard some as
stronger than others. Take for example the sermonic
point 'Every living body either grows, or dies; and so
does the soul'. And suppose we grant that every
living body either grows or dies. This conclusion
could with some confidence be transferred to plants,
for there are many and relevant resemblances between plants and animals. Could we apply it to a
star? The analogy is not close, but it may be instructive to think what we would mean by the 'growth' or
'death' of bodies astronomical, and one might,
having thought, come across some possible relationships between them which astronomers could try to
check. But can we speak of the soul as 'growing'?
Only by analogy. The metaphor cannot be
'cashed'.† We have no idea what it really
means. At most the analogy can convey to us a
conceivable relationship which may, or may not,
be appropriate to souls. The analogy has no
force at all. But it is a lively metaphor. It does
help us to go on talking about souls.

23   Is that a good thing? Or would it be
better, as positivists urge, to stop talking about
things we cannot explain or verify? That is a
wide point. It may be sufficient, having raised
this, to remark that theologians are not the only
people to deal in uncashable metaphors. Psycho-
logists do it too, and so do moralists, and
philosophers of language, including positivists. It
is some comfort, when caught offending, to

know that one offended in such bad company. 24   To conclude this excursus: analogies or comparisons are properly used to suggest possible similarities for further investigation. They may do this explicitly, spelling out a complex comparison in full, or implicitly, by proposing a conceptual model which carries such suggestions much as a metaphor does. An uncashable explicit analogy may, on a sufficiently interesting topic, be entertained *faute de mieux* as if it were an argument. Uncheckable implicit analogies are employed in several fields where we want to talk but do not really know what we are talking about (see XVI, *post*). One such field is theology.

XIII. Analogy Spoils Arguments

IF ALL theological terms are to be used 'subject to analogy', what effect will this have on our theology?
2   That depends of course on the nature of theology. The subject has traditionally been regarded as systematic and argumentative, an ordered presentation of what we know of God, with a structure of reasoning to connect the several parts, enabling us to move from one article to another round the web: a human science, deductive and precise, of the divine.
3   The material expounded in this book belongs to that theology: it is human, systematic, argumentative, and it relates to God, viz. the effect of his infinity on our talk of him. But the conclusion reached – that every theological statement is liable to qualification to an unknown and unspecifiable degree – destroys the whole subject. For propositions regarded as true only if appropriately (and incalculably) modified cannot usefully be constructed into arguments.
4   Such modification need not make prayer impossible. It is not nonsensical, when talking to someone, to add that he really knows better than we do what we mean. Every prayer could stand under a rubric 'please take this in the spirit intended even if the expression of it is unfortunate'. The 'Glory be to the Father, etc.,' often recited after psalms, has been expounded as 'Come back all I've said, if inappropriate': an afterthought some psalms need very

much. This constant qualification makes sense in the language of devotion because the person addressed is in a position to make the required allowances. It does not make sense in the language of theology, which is addressed to other people no better placed than the speaker to see what qualifications are required. It just will not do to propose an argument and then add in a reverent voice that both premisses and conclusion must be taken 'subject to analogy'.

5   It may be said that the conclusion is no worse off than the premisses, as the same qualifications have to be made to both; and that if the premisses are worth propounding even though mysterious, then the mysterious conclusion will be worth drawing too. But the question is, Can the conclusion be drawn, if we do not really understand the terms?

6   The force of any argument depends upon the statements within it *sharing the same terms*: for instance, what the conclusion refers to must also be referred to in the premisses. And it must be the *same* term in both places: not the same word meaning something different. If the meaning changes the argument will come unstuck. Obvious examples of this 'fallacy of four terms' are of course far from plausible; no children and very few adults would be taken in by

> No human beings are made of paper,
> All pages are made of paper,
> Therefore no human beings are pages.*

In a plausible example, conversely, the fallacy is less than obvious; but on reflection one can see that one term has been used in two slightly different ways:

> All metals are elements,

Brass is a metal,
Therefore brass is an element.

Here the term 'metal' is first used in the technical sense observed by chemists, and then in its wider common sense, which also covers what chemists call an alloy.† This argument is therefore said to fail for ambiguity.

7   To avoid the fallacy of ambiguity we must make sure each term is used in the same sense throughout the argument. Theological arguments contain terms 'subject to analogy', i.e. terms whose precise sense is unknown to those using them. Theologians, then, can never be sure of avoiding the fallacy of ambiguity in their arguments. Their readers are of necessity in the same unhappy plight. So while a theologian can propound what look like arguments, neither he nor his readers can possibly tell if they have any force. All theological reasoning herebelow is in practice *void for uncertainty*.

8   A theologian may claim that each of his terms is used in the same (though unknown) sense throughout his argument; so that, if the argument is formally correct, the conclusion is as certain as the premisses, though equally mysterious.

9   For some theological inferences this defence will not hold. These involve suppressed minor premisses acceptable only if we know the meaning of the terms. For instance, Descartes* and others have argued

God is good
∴ God is benevolent
∴ God will not deceive.

This involves two suppressed premisses

All good (conscious) beings are benevolent

No benevolent beings are deceivers

which appear self-evident if *good* and *benevolent* carry their ordinary sense. Whether they are true for beings 'good' or 'benevolent' in a different sense will depend upon that sense: if we can't make out their sense then we cannot tell whether they are true.

10   Suppose however we find a theological argument whose premises are fully stated and are acceptable, e.g. on grounds of some extrinsic guarantee, though their exact meaning cannot be properly expressed in human terms. Suppose further that the argument is formally valid, having a pattern like one of the approved samples in the logic-books. Can we then rely on the conclusion as true (though not fully comprehensible), on the grounds that the argument is in a valid form and the premises are guaranteed?

11   Some formal logicians would like to say Yes.* By way of persuasion they construct imaginary arguments containing nonsense-terms:

All shushful wugglies are glombular
All peridontic hepatites are shushful wugglies
Therefore all peridontic hepatites are glombular.

They claim (i) that we perceive the validity of such an argument, and that therefore (ii) the validity of an argument depends upon its form alone.

12   Claim (i) involves the assertion that it is impossible for the premises of the given 'argument' to be true while the conclusion remains false. This assertion is true in the very Pickwickian sense that neither premises nor conclusion can be either true or false, as all are meaningless.

13   Claim (ii) can survive the rejection of claim (i), for the notion of logical form can be explained

without appealing to nonsense-arguments. Given two sensible and valid arguments which are formally parallel:

All cows are mammals	All Frenchmen are Europeans
Some Friesians are cows	Some farmers are Frenchmen
∴ some Friesians are mammals	∴ some farmers are Europeans

we can readily identify the respect in which they are parallel and which accounts for their validity. And we can see that these arguments are valid before discovering whether the premisses are true. But can we recognize their validity in advance of *understanding* the premisses? Someone who did not know the meaning of *Friesian* could only say 'that *looks* a valid argument'.

14   Hume held that we could not trust reasoning outside the spheres of which we had experience; for we would not be able to tell when the argument was going wrong. He puts this most clearly in a comment on the philosophy of Malebranche, who believed that God did everything – not ultimately and indirectly, as 'first cause', but immediately and in person, using as mere 'occasions' for his work the people and bodies which seem to us to cause events. Hume puts his point in terms of his favourite game:

> Instead of saying that one billiard-ball moves another by a force which it has derived from the author of nature, it is the Deity himself, they say, who, by a particular volition, moves the second ball, being determined to this operation by the impulse of the first ball, in consequence of those general laws which he has laid down to himself in the government of the universe.

Hume replies that it is no good *arguing* a point like this:

> It seems to me that this theory of the universal energy and operation of the Supreme Being is too bold ever to carry conviction with it to a man, sufficiently apprized of the weakness of human reason, and the narrow limits to which it is confined in all its operations. Though the chain of arguments which conduct to it were ever so logical, there must arise a strong suspicion, if not an absolute assurance, that it has carried us quite beyond the reach of our faculties, when it leads to conclusions so extraordinary, and so remote from common life and experience. We are got into fairy land, long ere we have reached the last steps of our theory; and there we have no reason to trust our common methods of argument, or to think that our usual analogies and probabilities have any authority. Our line is too short to fathom such immense abysses. And however we may flatter ourselves that we are guided, in every step which we take, by a kind of verisimilitude and experience, we may be assured that this fancied experience has no authority when we thus apply it to subjects that lie entirely out of the sphere of experience.*

15   If Hume is right, as I believe he is, then an argument some of whose terms are to be taken subject to analogy cannot take us anywhere, except possibly to fairy land. Arguments of unknown meaning must be of inestimable value. And an inestimable argument is no damn use at all. All positive systematic theology is therefore void for uncertainty.

16   This danger was hinted at by Moses ben

Maimon of Cordoba, in his *Guide for the Perplexed*. To say that God knows, but not with a human wisdom etc., was, he said, very dangerous. It amounted to giving God a lot of unknown attributes.

> As for one who affirms an attribute of Him without knowing a thing about it except the mere term, it may be considered that the object to which he imagines the term applies is a nonexistent notion – an invention that is false; for he has, as it were, applied this term to a notion lacking existence, as nothing in existence is like that notion. An example is that of a man who has heard the term elephant and knows that it is an animal and demands to know its shape and true reality. Thereupon one who is himself mistaken or who misleads others tells him that it is an animal possessing one leg and three wings, inhabiting the depths of the sea, having a transparent body and a broad face like that of man in its form and shape, talking like a man, and sometimes flying in the air, while at other times swimming like a fish.*

Real Loch Ness theology!

17   Aquinas wished to avoid this agnostic result, and many of his followers are so sure he succeeded that they hardly mention it. Some even suppose that Aquinas' theory licenses theologians to carry on as if religious talk were in no way problematical and could be taken quite literally. Penido complains of

> . . some modern text-books, supposedly composed on Thomist lines (*ad mentem divi Thomae*). The section on 'divine names' makes a quick and sketchy curtsey to analogy, and passes on rapidly

to the next topic. What follows contains very few references to the initial doctrine. In theory it is taken for granted: our ideas about God are only 'analogous'. In spite of that there is, alas, a regular crop of univocal arguments.*

18   Thomas himself says repeatedly that we cannot know what God is – not even vaguely, inadequately, or 'non-quidditatively'. Denials apart, the best we can do is to use God's effects 'whether of nature or of grace, instead of any definition'. The terms we apply to God have a meaning which we cannot grasp, for they are

derived from our knowledge of his effects, not from our knowledge (or ignorance) of himself. 'Hence the perfection of all our knowledge about God is said to be a knowing of the unknown, for then supremely is our mind found to know God when it most perfectly knows that the being of God transcends everything whatever that can be apprehended in this life'.*

19   It is sometimes supposed that this limitation applies only to Natural Theology; though those who would honour God by decrying our natural capacities as sinful and inadequate rarely ask if such deficiencies might hamper their own proclamation of what they think God revealed. Thomas rightly rejects any special claims for 'Revelation' on this point.

Neither a Catholic nor a pagan knows the nature of God as it is in itself, but both know it only by way of some conception of causality, of transcendence or of negation. . . And although by the revelation, which is of grace, we do not know in this life what God is, and so can be united to him only

as one unknown to us, still it enables us to know
him more fully in so far as it displays to us both
more and better effects, and enables us to attribute to God certain things which are beyond the
scope of natural reason, such as that God is three
and one.*

20   The difference between Natural and Revealed
theology is simply a matter of where they get their
premisses. Natural Theology consists of those propositions about God that can be inferred from statements that any reasonable person will accept, e.g.
that some things move. Revealed Theology contains
further propositions, not derivable from these, but
contained in or deducible from some special set of
statements accepted as revealed, i.e. (presumably)
guaranteed by God. The divine guarantee extends
only to the truth of these propositions. It does not
make them any easier to understand.

21   I have argued that if the meaning of statements
about God is uncertain then no arguments based
upon these statements can be known to hold. This
inference applies equally wherever we got the statements from. Revealed theology, as Thomas saw, is
no more intelligible than the 'natural' variety; nor, I
add, is it any more reliable.

22   Thomas, who spent much of his life collecting
and arranging arguments about God, presumably
did not then think them all void for uncertainty. In
1273, however, he stopped writing, and more or less
stopped talking too, saying when pressed 'all I have
hitherto written seems to me nothing but straw . . .
compared to what I have seen and what has been
revealed to me'.* It is tempting to read our own
meaning into this, and say the penny had dropped
at last, Thomas had seen through it all. Spurning

this temptation – for what Thomas 'saw' may have been quite different – let us concentrate on what we can see, without any special sanctity or unusual aid: that arguments whose terms are uncertain are without probative effect.

23   The theology this argument debunks is not just natural, or just revealed, nor is it only the orthodox varieties preached from pulpits and retailed in seminaries of divinity. It is not something peculiar to Theologians, or for that matter to Logicians either. It is not just Other People's. *Everyone* engages in theology. For everyone – including philosophers who call theology nonsense and preachers who reject 'propositional' theology – everyone holds some beliefs about the ultimate nature of the universe, and makes some inferences from those beliefs. If the terms used in stating those beliefs are subject to analogy then none of the inferences can be known to hold. Berkeley, as usual, has it in a nutshell: 'You cannot argue from unknown attributes, or, which is the same thing, from attributes in an unknown sense.†

24   It is sometimes suggested that we can safely argue from any one theological model or analogy so long as we qualify our conclusion by striking out whatever conflicts with the consequences of any other model, analogy or metaphor. Bethune-Baker explains this rather vital point, in a footnote not very early in the book:

> Arius seems, in part at least, to have been misled by a wrong use of analogy, and by mistaking description for definition. All attempts to explain the nature and relations of the Deity must largely depend on metaphor, and no one metaphor can exhaust those relations. Each metaphor can only

describe one aspect of the nature or being of the Deity, and the inferences which can be drawn from it have their limits when they conflict with the inferences which can be truly drawn from other metaphors describing other aspects. From one point of view Sonship is a true description of the inner relations of the Godhead: from another point of view the title Logos describes them best. Each metaphor must be limited by the other. The title Son may obviously imply later origin and a distinction amounting to ditheism. It is balanced by the other title Logos, which implies co-eternity and inseparable union. Neither title exhausts the relations. Neither may be pressed so far as to exclude the other.*

25   This salvaging explanation neither explains nor salvages. First, can *any* metaphor be used to draw inferences about Deity? Or are we restricted to those in the Bible (plus a few that the Fathers were rather partial to)? Second, the difficulty is not so much that no single analogy can say enough about God, but that each of them – to judge by its conflicts with the others – implies too much. Ah, says Bethune-Baker, but there's safety in numbers. The inferences drawn

. . .

> have their limits when they conflict with the inferences which can be truly drawn from other metaphors . . .

Then which do we give up? If we take him literally, both: 'neither may be pressed so far as to exclude the other'. In practice he will pick and choose, keeping 'the equality in kind' that *Son* suggests but dropping the 'later origin', keeping the 'co-eternity' hinted at by *Logos* but dropping the 'dependence' or 'emanation' which that metaphor implies. But if after an argument we still have to decide *on other grounds* which of its conclusions to accept, why not make do with those other grounds and drop the argument? An inference *some* of whose conclusions may turn out to be acceptable is like 'In case of complaint please return to the manufacturer' stencilled on a parachute. In effect, Bethune-Baker is saying that the various official metaphors are to be taken as suggestive analogies *and not as arguments*; which could have been said in larger print, and on page one, for it is a fundamental re-writing of the long sad story of Christian theology.

26   In those 39 Articles agreed upon (so the title-page tells us)

> by the Archbishops and Bishops of both provinces and the whole clergy in the Convocation holden at London in the year 1562

Article VI reads thus:

> Holy Scripture containeth all things necessary to salvation: so that whatsoever is not read therein, nor may be proved thereby, is not to be required of any man, that it should be believed as an article of the faith, or be thought requisite or necessary to salvation.

27   The intention of this article is clearly negative: priests are not to lay down *extra* beliefs as a condition for entry into heaven. But the phrase 'nor may be proved' readmits all the dogmas, and disputes, of traditional argumentative theology. If this phrase were omitted, in view of the agnostic consequence of the theory of analogy, all non-Biblical dogmas (e.g. the Trinity) and all inferred teachings whatsoever (e.g. 'thou shalt not bear false witness to the Inland

Revenue') would have to be struck out of the small print on the back of the ticket. For to say that salvation depends on acceptance of Scripture *and of what follows from it* is to assume either that we can tell for certain what does follow, or that God will not only look after his text but will also guarantee inferences whose validity we cannot see. The evidence of Christian history tells, on the whole, against this latter assumption. The theory of analogy makes the former one untenable.

28   The abolition of argumentative theology should make the list of 'saving beliefs' shorter and less systematic. It will also undermine the unscriptural notion of a *list* of 'saving beliefs'. Is religion reduced to devotion, then? Or can there also be theology of some other, non-argumentative variety? I shall try to answer these questions later in the book.

29   Having now reached the main point – that arguments subject to analogy are unusable – it may be helpful to re-capitulate the argument so far: (i) The way religious people talk seems queer, and needs interpretation, (ii) as one would expect, seeing how they compare with that of which they speak. (iii) One line of interpretation is offered in the classic theory of analogy, (iv) which applies to all positive statements about God, (v) and is based on the analogy, or similarity, a creature must bear to its creator. (vi) The theory must apply to all terms applied to God, and should say that any or all of them *may* need qualification. (vii) Applied to terms already irreducible, it says that we can't know what they mean. (viii) The theory cannot tell us what they do mean, but encourages us to soldier on in ignorance. (ix) It cannot be established by means of argument, but is acceptable without. (x) The 'analogy' of the theory is related (by analogy) to

common-or-garden 'argument by analogy'. (xi) The theory, if taken seriously, must destroy argumentative theology.

30   Before examining this fatal consequence let us look briefly at some objections and alternatives.

5. Some Objections to the Theory

XIV. Contextual Determination of Meaning

WE BEGAN our enquiry by asking how the ordinary meaning of a term is affected when it is put to special and religious use. Some would call this approach misguided. It is wrong, they would say, to think that words mean something first, *in vacuo* (or in a dictionary), and that this official meaning is then qualified for use on special occasions. It is the use, on any occasion, that gives the meaning of the word.* A dictionary tries to distil this meaning from the commoner contexts of its use, but there is nothing 'proper' or 'official' about this general or central use. Every (established) usage is as good as another. None are nonsense. None are deviants.

2   Those who say this appear to hold that the meaning is *fully* determined by the use. The notion that one could be saying something, but without knowing precisely what, strikes them as nonsensical. 'Whatever can be said, can be said clearly'.†

3   On this view, the apparently otiose task of expounding a certain use (for instance the use of *father* in addressing God), can be carried out only 'from within' that 'language-game'. The introduction of external criteria of meaning or intelligibility is therefore illegitimate. For instance, scientists may decide not to consider theories which are beyond the control of experiment and experience: but to demand such verification in a discussion of a

piece of music would just show oneself a Philistine. Each context is self-regulating and autonomous.

4   This ruling has been employed in the instruction of anthropologists. When studying another culture (these people say) he must not apply to it the categories he brought with him on the plane. It will not do, for instance, to describe as illogical the mode of thought of a tribe we call 'primitive'. For, as one writer puts it:

> Criteria of logic are not a direct gift of God, but arise out of, and are only intelligible in the context of, ways of living or modes of social life. It follows that one cannot apply criteria of logic to modes of social life as such. For instance, science is one such mode and religion is another: and each has criteria of intelligibility peculiar to itself . . . we cannot sensibly say that either the practice of science itself or that of religion is either illogical or logical; both are non-logical.*

This writer feels it must be wrong for an outsider to describe certain tribal beliefs about witchcraft as *incorrect*: not because they are right, but because he is an outsider, there.* The most he may properly say is that such beliefs are untenable in Manchester or Birmingham.

5   The local religion(s) in Birmingham and Manchester can also be immunised against linguistic doubt by this line of argument. The doubt arose from noticing the non-literal character of much religious talk. Some inferred that all of it must be nonsensical. Religion, they said, was a product of linguistic confusions. It was all a big mistake. But (asks the language-game theorist) how could you discover the mistake? Have you an *independent* concept of reality, above all particular contexts and free

from the limitations of each, by which to measure religion and declare it unsatisfactory? The concepts of reality, intelligibility, and explanation are internal to the language-games in which they are applied, and are not available for use outside. If religion, or science, is a going concern, a form of life that people live, a language-game, then it cannot be criticised or debunked wholesale.

6   Archimedes said 'Give me a standing-point and I will move the world'. The modern astronomy says that there are no such points. Each circling sphere is a world to itself, a centre of attraction, and each acts on all the other spheres; but our everyday terrestrial notion of a *terra firma*, from which all actions are measured and in which firm foundations can be always sunk, has no application in the sky. So even with a lever long enough and strong enough Archimedes could not move the world.

7   Each language-game, on the view we are considering, is an independent world. There are no fixed points outside them all from which logical leverage could be applied to dislodge one or another language-world and send it crashing through the void.

8   These arguments depend rather heavily on the analogies they introduce. Let us try to cash them, and see if – on 'surrender values' – the position is still firm.

9   Is religion or science a *world*, a separate system of life circling in empty logical space at unbridgeable distances from the other worlds? No, the traffic between them all is heavy and continuous. None of the departments of life could exist entirely on its own. There may be special rules and forms to be observed in each: but all are part, for each participant, of his own single life. Making the distinctions absolute would lead to a sort of schizophrenia.

10   Is religion or science a *game*, played strictly by its own set rules, and which anyone can play once he learns 'how to carry on', even if he sees no point in it or them? No, religion and science are serious occupations, and the force and point of their special forms and rules derive in the end from the serious business of living that common human life to which they both belong. Religion claims to tell us how to live that life. That claim deserves our attention. It is in the detailed working-out of such a 'serious and devout call' that one might be persuaded to cover the head in prayer, or not to play cards on Sundays, or always to bow before the Sacrament. Apart from the meaning of religion for our life such observances would become mere flummery. Science, again, is hardly an esoteric pastime. We may treasure a caricature of the abstracted, long-haired scientist who cannot eat lunch because his false teeth have got tangled up in some footling and pointless experiment. But that is not true to life. Science is a sustained and concerted attempt to find out exactly how things are and what makes them work. By its aid we make steel ships and telephones and aeroplanes, predict the tides and control malaria. And these things matter very much to us.

11   Do science and religion nevertheless resemble games in making their own rules and having a specialised vocabulary? Yes. Are those rules and vocabulary beyond correction from outside? That depends what 'outside' means. It is the relation between these specialised pursuits and ordinary life, and the corresponding relation between their specialised lingoes and ordinary talk, that is under discussion. This question must not be begged by appeal to analogies like 'autonomy' or 'game', for the question is whether these analogies apply.

12   The clearest instances of formal systems of thought with fully explicit rules, which seemingly debar appeal to anything outside, are found in the mathematics. But even here ordinary language has to be used (as 'meta-language') in setting up the rules, and some basic concepts are 'regarded as primitive', i.e. taken on loan with no questions asked. It may also be urged that what goes on inside the system, if justified solely by the rules, is not really *inference*.

> . . . the mathematician, in so far as he really is 'playing a game' *draws no conclusions*. For in this context 'playing' must mean *proceeding* in accordance with certain rules. And to draw the conclusion that proceeding in such and such a way would accord with the general rule is itself to go beyond mere play . . . it is essential to mathematics that its symbols are also employed *in mufti*. It is the use outside mathematics, i.e. the *meaning* of the symbols that makes mathematics out of symbol-play.*

13   The same, I suggest, applies to religion and to science. Each has its terminology and rituals, intelligible only to enthusiasts. But the point of either 'form of life' depends on its relation to ordinary life: and the significance (meaning and importance) of their technical terms depends similarly on a series of possible explanations ('definitions') linking them back to an everyday language already understood. For religion (or science) is not a form of life in the sense that carbon 214 is a form of carbon: it is more like a department or aspect of life. Only for a special few is it bread-and-butter too, and family, and diversion and recreation for the intellect. And the technical sub-language of, say, Christian theology

no more constitutes *a language* than do the terminology of set theory or the terms of musical dynamics
or the 'language of flowers': it is just a collection of
terms given limited and precise meanings for use in
that speciality.

14   So far we have discussed whether religion, or
science (or public relations or accountancy or chess
. . .) are properly regarded as autonomous forms of
life each with a separate language of its own. If the
answer is *no*, then it may become possible to dismiss
chess as trivial or public relations as disingenuous –
or a religion as incoherent. It will not establish that
religion *is* incoherent; but only that someone who
says it is cannot be simply dismissed as unintelli-
gent. We may have to look and see if there is anything in what he says. These are very general points
concerning the nature of explanation and intelligibility. But the thesis we are considering states that the
meaning of *every* word is determined by its use. Does
this mean that each particular context settles the
meanings of the terms that come into it? Or does
'use' mean 'usage' in a more general and public
sense?

15   It is clear, first of all, that most of us first come
across most terms *in use*, and go seeking a definition,
if at all, only after comprehending something of
what that term was on that occasion used to mean.
We do not often learn meanings from definitions.
Systems of thought presented *axiomatically* (definitions first) are in fact very difficult to understand.
What a definition does is to *define*, to draw precise
lines around a meaning we have already vaguely
grasped.

16   A second point is that we commonly say things
twice, one way or another. Ordinary language is
highly 'redundant', as is gratefully acknowledged by

cable and wireless engineers. It is rare for a mistake of one letter, even in a telegram, to alter or destroy the sense. Because of this, textual critics can detect the 'corruption' by mis-copying of an ancient text, and can often restore with confidence what the original writer *must have* said. In the same way expert readers of literatures now very incomplete (such as Homer, or the Bible) can often work out the meaning of a word of unknown etymology and occurring only once.

17 Often, but not always. For some contexts 'supply' the missing word much more readily than others do. In an addition sum we can actually work it out:

$$2 + 5 + 3 + \qquad +6 = 20$$

On a Roman tombstone we can expect to find the usual formulae. Sometimes, however, we can only guess the category of the missing word; in

She was wearing a   gaberdine raincoat

the blank could well have held a colour-word, though we can't at all tell which, but it might have had *belted*, *fashionable* or *knee-length*. At the other extreme, gaps in snippets of poetry in crossword clues are usually, alas!, unfillable on general principles. One has got to remember what the poem actually said.

18 The examples most favourable to this theory occur in games. *Silly-mid-off* denotes a particular position on the cricket field, and one can perfectly well learn the position without knowing how he got that name. A *pawn* is a chess-piece that moves one space forwards at a time. You learn this by learning chess, not by studying pawnshops and then applying the theory of analogy. The same could be said of

boundary, *long-stop* and *king*: could be, but is usually not. In these, as in most more serious cases, ways of speaking are not insulated from each other in mutually exclusive systems of rules. What can be said in one context by the use of a certain expression depends for its sense on the use of that expression in other contexts (other language-games).

19   The religious context – not just the rest of the sentence, but the whole occasion and atmosphere, with the customs and institutions and memories involved – this context does subtly qualify the way we take the terms. And one can grasp this effect without knowing anything of the theory of analogy. But the effect is one of qualification, of the special occasion modifying the ordinary, standard use. This can be seen from expository works, which commonly proceed by pointing out the literal (ordinary, regular, standard) meaning of the terms in some doctrine and then adding the qualifications needed for the doctrine to make religious sense.

20   This work of interpretation is notoriously subject to dispute. The expositor himself 'just sees' that the words mean one thing; his critic 'feels in his bones' that they mean something else. Unable to establish or confute either point by publicly acceptable reasoning they humanly turn to shouting and abuse. This makes it of some importance to distinguish such religious interpretation from philosophical analysis.

21   By 'interpretation' I mean the commending of alternative ways of putting what a religious (or literary) text is thought to say. 'Analysis' I take in this context to be the exploration of how such interpretations work. The discussions in the present book are intended as a contribution to analysis. But if someone says that the real meaning of Christ's

'rising from the dead' was the new-found openness to the future which his disciples experienced after Pentecost,* he is (I say) offering an interpretation of the phrase 'he rose again'.

22   It is common ground among such interpreters of creeds that the terms there used do not really mean what they plainly seem to say, but something else. Having thought of his something else, and found religious value there, the interpreter may well suppose that he is engaging in analysis, in laying bare the 'depth grammar' of the phrase 'he rose again' and exposing what it really means, as Russell engaged in analysis when he replaced 'Scott was the author of *Waverley*' by 'one and only one man wrote *Waverley*, and that man was Scott', and then ('more fully') by

> There is an entity c such that the statement 'x wrote *Waverley*' is true if x is c and false otherwise: moreover c is Scott.*

There is no harm in calling these proposed equivalents 'analyses'. But religious interpretations are not simply equivalent to the phrases interpreted, or they would occasion less dispute. They are revised versions, not explanations, of their originals.

23   The distinction I wish to draw could also be stated in terms of reducible symbols and those that we cannot see behind (VII. 1, *ante*). 'Scott was the author of Waverley' can be reduced (if that is the right word) to 'one and only one man wrote Waverley, and that man was Scott'. And in some cases a reductive analysis can be given of religious terms: perhaps 'descended into Hell' *just* means 'somehow gave the dead a chance'. But every religious system has some symbols that we cannot see behind. These irreducibles can be interpreted,

mainly by suggesting the area of human existence in which they are 'at home'; thus one may well say that the practical meaning to Christ's disciples of what they called his Resurrection consisted in their own new way of facing life. This is valuable as a (possible) 'location' of the credal phrase. To take it as a reduction is perhaps simple minded.* To take it as analysis is ignorant.

24   To summarise: we first learn words *in use*, getting the general drift from the rest of the sentence and then filling in the meaning-gap. There are some holes in sentences which only one peg will fit: some holes will take several, of similar shape: some will accept a large variety. But if the same peg is fitted into several different holes they will together determine it quite closely. Presented with several sentences containing the same unknown word an intelligent listener can usually hit upon their common element. He can then explain it, to himself or another, in a *definition*, which states *and limits* the meaning of the term.

25   The specialised vocabularies – of farming, or fishing, or philosophy – arise partly by the invention of new words used only in that sphere, but mainly by further restriction or precise specification, for that particular purpose, of the meaning of some common term. Such a definition creates a *technical term*. Thus a *salt*, for chemists, may be defined as 'a substance produced by the replacement of the whole or of part of the hydrogen of an acid by a metal – thus defining a whole class of substances which in this structural way resemble common salt.† You might think you know what makes a car 'automatic', and yet find it difficult to state. To put the difference technically: ' "Vehicle with automatic transmission" means a vehicle in which the driver is

not provided with any means whereby he may, independently of the use of the accelerator or the brakes, vary gradually the proportion of the power being produced by the engine which is transmitted to the road wheels of the vehicle'.*

26 Theology has many technical terms and very few new words. The language of devotion has next to none of either; for someone who sets out to formulate a strict definition of *prayer* or *almighty* or *resurrection* is already engaging in theology. Many users of these religious terms are quite aware that they bear a special sense and use them correctly in that sense, though they might not be able to frame a formal definition nor have time for discussions such as these.

27 In a living, growing, synthesising activity (like religion) usage is the only norm. To find out what people mean by *soul* we must wait and see how they use the word when no one is watching and they are not trying to be 'correct'. In a parasitic, academic, analytic study (like theology) definition is to be encouraged and even stipulation is allowed, if only the stipulator sticks to it.

28 It is true that 'the meaning is the use'. It is not often true, as a matter of linguistic history, that the meaning in one type of context has arisen quite independently of the usage of that same word elsewhere (if it were true often, we should have to revise our notion of *that word*). Even if a specialised meaning is learnt independently, as though it were a new word, the best way to explain it to others is usually by modification of the general meaning found 'in ordinary use'. And this is the method commonly followed in explaining terms of religion and theology.

29 I conclude that no valid objection to the theory

of analogy can be drawn from theories of meaning employing the slogan 'look to the use'.

xv. Family Resemblances

In expounding the theory of analogy we took it for granted that a term common to all the contexts of its ordinary use would normally have a single and clearly defined meaning. Some now regard this traditional view as a mistake. If it is mistaken, then the theory of analogy is probably useless, and superfluous. It will not explain the peculiar religious use of terms; indeed, there may be nothing peculiar in religious usage for it to explain.

2   On the traditional view, each thing to which a term applies possesses certain qualities, some of which – and the same ones, in each – are what that term 'connotes' or means. The meaning or 'essence' of a term can thus be clearly defined, either by listing all the qualities to which it universally refers, or more briefly by giving another term connoting most of them (the 'genus' or family term) and then finishing off the specification with the qualities peculiar to that particular term (the 'difference'). Thus a *triangle* may be defined as a plane figure with three straight sides, or more briefly as a three-sided polygon; and *man* was traditionally held to be a *rational animal*.

3   There are of course all sorts and conditions of men. Some are tall, some short: some are dark, some fair: some are clever, some are not. The definition leaves out all these 'accidental' qualities: for whatever else each of them may be, taken for all in all, he

is a man. The term refers only, and always, to those qualities which are common to humanity. Let us call this traditional view the 'single-essence theory': for it says that each term has one essence, one set of qualities separately necessary and jointly sufficient for a thing to merit the application of that term.

4   It has lately been urged that this view does not fit all the facts. In our actual usage of the word *game* no single common feature or features can be found, it is said, uniting all the instances:

> Don't say there *must* be something common to them, otherwise they would not be called 'games' – but *look* whether anything is common to them all – for, if you look at them, you will not see anything common to *all*, but you will see similarities and relationships, a whole row of them. As I said: don't think, look! – look at board-games, for instance, with their various relationships. Now go on to card-games: here you find many correspondences with that first set, but many common features disappear, and others appear. If we now go on to ball-games, a certain amount of the common element remains, but much is lost. Are they all *entertaining*?
> Compare chess with noughts and crosses. Does winning and losing always come in? Do the players always compete? Think of patience. In ball-games winning and losing do occur, but if a child throws a ball against a wall and catches it again, this element has disappeared. See what part luck plays, and where skill comes into it. And how different skill in chess is from skill in tennis. Then think of games like ring-a-ring-o'-roses: the element of entertainment occurs here, but how many of the other characteristics have disappeared!

And we could go on like this through many, many other groups of games, seeing how similarities turn up and disappear.

The result of this investigation is, that we see a complicated net of similarities, overlapping and cutting across one another, large and small scale similarities.

The best word I can find to characterise these similarities is 'family-resemblances': for the various similarities which occur between members of a family overlap and cut across like this: figure, facial features, colour of eyes, walk, temperament, etc. etc. And I shall say 'games form a family'.*

5   This writer applied his suggestion to 'languages' or 'language-games' in his idiosyncratic sense: the language of chess, the language of architecture, etc. etc. Others have applied it to concepts thought philosophically basic (and indefinable) such as *knowledge*, *explanation*, and *intelligence*. On the traditional, single-essence view one could sensibly ask 'What is knowledge?', and – finding no one answer – feel puzzled and profound, for there *must*, on that view, be something common to all the items denoted by that term. On the family-resemblance theory there need not be. Though clearly there still *can* be. Chess, for instance, is strictly and officially defined. And the writer himself, in the passage quoted, looks for a term to 'characterise' the examples he investigates, i.e. to hit off the features he has found common and peculiar to them all. So terms allegedly applied in the family way are not themselves alleged to form a family.

6   All the 'family' analogy shows is that a classification by features would not correspond with one by

blood-relationship, and that a classification by one feature ('all blue-eyed boys over here') might cut across that by another ('all long-haired uncles over there'). But it is common ground that if we classify on several bases at once, muddle will probably result.

7   The main instance, *game*, is shown to be very various, though most of its separate instances are clearly defined. Does it show then that a super-grouping or *genus* (= family) may be very wide? But that is hardly news.

8   The example is carefully chosen. It is meant as a challenge. The author denies that the single-essence theory holds universally, and to prove his point he challenges the single-essence theorist to find the single essence common to all games. There is, he claims, no one feature or set of features to be found in everything we call a game and sufficient to justify our application of the term.

9   He may well be right. Our usage is often rather loose. Even where a term has a strict and settled meaning – such as 'uncle' – we often apply it to individuals who lack one or another defining feature but still have enough to be more like an uncle than like anything else that comes to mind. It was said of F.H. Bradley that he called his Absolute 'God' because he coudn't think what the devil else to call it. Our experience is often more various than our immediate vocabulary: so – if nothing much is at stake – we stretch a point and call it by the nearest handy name.

10   These names have a way of sticking: so the meanings of many words gradually grow, branching out in various directions, until it is true (of a few) that no single essence can be found common to all the various meanings of the word. The unity in such

a case is purely historical, and may be left to lexico-graphers.

11 Is it in fact true that there is no feature common to all games? That hardly seems to matter, now we've got the point. There is very likely no external-ly describable element – such as competition, spe-cial dress, or fun – to be found in all; just as there is no single type of activity which a farmer must, to be a farmer, always carry on.* But in that case the true definition is relational. Farming is making a living by raising crops and/or rearing animals. Very various activities may on various occasions contri-bute to that end, though no one runs through them all. Teaching again may be defined as professionally helping others learn. As there are all sorts of ways and means of doing that, so all sorts of doings and thinkings will at one time or another count as *teach-ing* and there is no single type of doing or thinking which has to be present in each one.

12 Following these examples, we could define *play-ing a game* as 'doing something according to a set of rules but without further and serious intent'.

13 Will this definition cover every single thing you or I or the man on the Clapham omnibus would be ready to hear called a game? Very likely not. So much depends on where you want to draw the line. There will always be debatable cases, and the debating of them consists of proposing places at which to draw the line, proposals another debater can always reject if he has a mind. The debating of cases does not however show line-drawing to be futile or impossible, but enjoyable and popular.

14 To avoid debate at this point let us concede that there may be some words whose several senses are in common use so very various that no single thread can be found running through them all. Such

words clearly would not lend themselves to being singly and unambiguously defined. To describe them adequately one would need to distinguish and list several different senses, and perhaps to trace or guess the stretchings and branchings by which one sense grew from another in the past. Which is what dictionaries do, and have done for a century or two.

15   This discovery has no immediate reference to the defining of terms. A term is a man-made item, deliberately delimited for some special purpose such as argument. As arguments become doubtful if ambiguous it is necessary to limit each term in them to a single sense: which is done by listing, in a definition, those features that are necessary and sufficient for correct application of the term.

16   A term is specially made to bear a single sense. There is no more need to 'postulate' univocity in terms than to postulate that a chair has legs. It is pointless to suggest 'stretching a point' or 'looking at usage' if the term is to fulfil its function in an argument: it is like asking a boxer to put his hands in his pockets like the others in the crowd.

17   I conclude that recent discussions of 'family resemblances' between the various senses of a word do not undermine or render superfluous or – as one writer suggests – replace the theory of analogy.* It is no comfort to the atheist to learn that poker, the game, has nothing in common with the poker used to poke the fire. What he wants to hear is what *is* common in meaning between 'Dad' said at home and 'Our Father' said in prayer.

XVI. Borrowing

THE THEORY says ordinary terms must be modified in meaning when borrowed for theological purposes. I say that (unless the modification is precisely specified) this precludes their honest use in argument (XIII). Two objections to this have been considered: that the terms are not borrowed (and therefore never modified), but grow spontaneously and independently in each separate field of use (XIV); and that there need be no single essential and proper meaning of a term (XV). I must now meet a third objection; that as everyone does it, even scientists, it must be quite all right.

2   That terms are borrowed, and put to new uses, is hardly in dispute. We speak of electric *resistance*, and *current*; of light *waves*, and *escaping* gas; of *repression* and the *sub-conscious*, of *depressions* (over the Atlantic) and a *rise* in temperature; of a *spark* of genius, a *storm* of passion and the *ebbing* of desire. Each of these terms has a proper, original setting-in-life: and it means what it means when borrowed for analogy or metaphor because of what it originally meant in its proper place. A team can hardly play 'away' unless it has a *home* away from which to play.

3   Some think these analogies harmful and dispensable. Nothing, says George Berkeley

> seems more to have contributed towards engaging men in controversies and mistakes, with regard to

the nature and operations of the mind, than the being used to speak of those things in terms borrowed from sensible ideas. For example, the will is termed the motion of the soul: this infuses a belief, that the mind of man is as a ball in motion, impelled and determined by the objects of sense, as necessarily as that is by the stroke of a racket. Hence arise endless scruples and errors of dangerous consequence in morality. All which, I doubt not, may be cleared, and truth appear plain, uniform, and consistent, could but philosophers be prevailed on to retire into themselves, and attentively consider their own meaning.*

4   It is probably bad if words stop us thinking what we mean. And if we can express that meaning *properly*, with unborrowed terms, in words that play 'at home' (to give two very metaphorical indications of what we mean by *properly*) then it is probably better just to say what we mean instead of saying something else. Metaphor will be justified only for temporary and special purposes, like illustration, advertisement or emphasis. But in some cases we have to borrow terms in order even to say what we mean. In some areas of life we live on linguistic credit all the time.

5   If we can say the very same thing in proper terms then no philosophical problem arises. Mistake and fallacy can be avoided, as Berkeley thought, simply by self-discipline. This is true in some sicientific contexts where theory *replaces* the analogy that helped in working out the theory. It is, for example, unnecessary to go on thinking of gravitation as a *pull*, when the equations of motion have once been made out and verified. Electrical theory would not be less effective or complete if we

replaced *current* and *resistance* by newly-invented terms, though it might in that case be a little more difficult to learn. These ladders *can* be thrown away once we are standing on the wall. The paper money is held because it can be cashed at any time for real gold.

6 Some borrowings have not yet acquired this empirical cash-value, because a precise and quantitative theory has yet to be worked out. In these areas the borrowing of terms is at present unavoidable; and it seems to each borrower that the terms he has borrowed are indispensable. Conflicting schools may then grow up (as in psychology), unable to talk to each other because each sees the other's terms as unlicensed borrowings, mere metaphors, inappropriate analogies.

7 It may be that in some such fields a quantitative and verifiable theory is for ever unattainable, so the borrowings will never acquire cash-value in that way. But until someone proves this we have no way of telling which loans are simply immature and which, like Consols, irredeemable. Until we can draw that distinction in practice there is little point in theorising separately on irredeemables. Both immature and irredeemable loans have no *present* cash value. What limitations does that place upon their use?

8 The borrowed terms are used in arguments. They must be, in order to work out the theories one of which, it is hoped, will one day redeem the borrowing. They are used 'speculatively', we could say, or 'in theorising'. In this use they may, but need not, be qualified. For instance, no psychiatrist will draw a line on the head below which the sub-conscious is supposed to start; and a cautious psychiatric theorist will not use the term in theorising in a way that

depends on this spatial aspect of the analogy. But not all theorists are cautious. And quite often no one knows what qualifications are required – that may be why we are still speculating in that field.

9   It appears then that if not everyone, at least some others (including scientists), are doing what I say is improper when done by theologians. They are using borrowed terms whose meaning requires unspecified (or unspecifiable) qualification; and they are using them in arguments. Does this mean the theologians are not as bad as I made out: or that some scientists are worse?

10   If no one were ever allowed to use a borrowed term in argument until the meaning was completely specified, it would probably have been impossible to work out the quantitative theories whose verification has in some cases specified the meaning completely and thus matured the loan. If borrowing were stopped speculation would soon grind to a halt. Instead of issuing general (and unenforceable) prohibitions, as the positivists did, it is better simply to point out that the terms *are* borrowed, and that until the theory is complete and verified the whole construction must be taken with a grain of salt. It's 'only theorising': a valuable activity when rightly directed, but while still in progress completely hypothetical.

11   Theologians have not in the past been prepared to admit that their grandiose systems were 'only theorising' and completely hypothetical. The defence that 'scientists do it too' (viz. borrow terms) would be available to a theologian (i) if he would regard his own results as speculations, rather than established truths, and agree that the different speculations of others had an equal claim to devout and serious consideration; and (ii) if he could say what

possible public and practical results he would regard as confuting his theory, and what as tending to confirm it*.

6. Reforming Theology to Suit the Theory

XVII. Dogmatic Systems

THEOLOGY has traditionally been regarded as a systematic presentation of our knowledge about God. The system in question is a logical one: some items are presented as deriving from others by means of arguments. And some at least of the knowledge is dependent on these arguments: some statements are presented as reliable *because of* their logical derivation from other statements already guaranteed.

2   This view of the nature of theology is so generally taken for granted that it is not often explicitly stated or discussed. The following statement of it would have been acceptable to most theologians in most centuries and in most compartments of the church:

> The foundations, then, having been laid in the most solid way, there is needed, further, a use of philosophy, both perpetual and manifold, in order that Sacred Theology may assume and put on the nature, habit and character of true science. For in this noblest kind of learning it is above everything necessary that the parts of heavenly doctrine, being many and different, should be gathered together, as it were, into one body. Thus they are united by a union of harmony among themselves, all the parts being fittingly arranged, and derived from their own proper principles.

Lastly all of these parts, and each of them, must be strengthed by unanswerable arguments suited to each case.*

This account fits the theology of Barth in this century or of Robert Barclay, the Quaker, in the seventeenth, as well as it fits Aquinas in the thirteenth century or Augustine in the fifth.

3   Now IF theology is such a descriptive and argumentative science of the divine, THEN (I have argued) the theory of analogy if accepted and thoroughly thought through will make all its inferences void for uncertainty.

4   But not *all* theology, the Thomist will say, is symbolic in the sense required. Some terms, like *rock* or *lion*, are indeed applied to God by way of metaphor; and from statements containing them no further inferences can be safely drawn. But some terms – *being*, for instance, and *living, wise* and *good* – are said of him properly (or 'literally') without any transference or metaphor, for we do not merely wish to say that God has some resemblance to a good man, nor just that he is the cause of goodness in others; we say that he really is good.* And it is what we wish to say that counts. It is the ordinary religious sense of men that their religious language must express, not a sophisticated alternative dreamt up by theologians. On this point the Thomist would agree with the spirit, at least, of Mill's protest against Mansel:

I will call no being good who is not what I mean when I apply that epithet to my fellow-creatures; and if such a being can sentence me to hell for not so calling him, to hell I will go.*

5   Now it is these 'literal' (i.e. non-metaphorical)

terms that are said to be subject to analogy. Yet,
says Thomas,

> although we never use words in exactly the same
> sense of creatures and God we are not merely
> equivocating when we use the same word . . . for
> if this were so we could never argue from state-
> ments about creatures to statements about God –
> any such argument would be invalidated by the
> Fallacy of Equivocation. That this does not
> happen we know not merely from the teachings of
> the philosophers who prove many things about
> God but also from the teaching of St. Paul . . . We
> must say, therefore, that words are used of God
> and creatures in an analogical way.*

6   Thomas grants, in this passage, that argument is
essential to theology and that ambiguity is very bad
for arguments. But theology, he says, is a science: so
it cannot be that our terms mean something quite
different when applied to God. This inference could
be compared with a well-known one of Kant's: that
since geometry is a science its object, Space, cannot
be something whose properties we have gathered by
observation in the course of our experience.* But
who says geometry is a real science, or theology?
Such an argument is the wrong way round. It begs
the question we are trying to discuss.
7   I say that analogy is almost as bad for arguments
as is outright ambiguity. If a term means something
partly different when applied to God, and if we
cannot say how different its meaning then becomes,
then any argument in which it plays a part is unre-
liable *for us*. Then I argue (the right way round) that
as terms are applied to God herebelow only by analogy, argumentative theology cannot exist as a
descriptive science.

8   Several alternatives open before us at this point. If the acceptance that theological terms are subject to analogy involves the abandonment of argumentative theology as a descriptive science of God, we could decide either

(A) not to accept that theological terms are subject to analogy,

or (B) to abandon religion as well as theology,

or (C) to continue religion without any theology,

or (D) to continue religion with a non-argumentative descriptive theology,

or (E) to continue religion each with his private theology,

or (F) to continue religion with a public but non-descriptive theology.

9   A full discussion of these alternatives would be matter for another book. Here I shall pass a few remarks on the first five alternatives and then say a little to commend the sixth.

XVIII. Five Ways Nowhere

(A) LITERALISM

If theological terms are not subject to analogy they are presumably to bear their ordinary sense. We could call this *literalism*, but it is not the only sort. It is not the naïve literalism of the man who has never considered what sort of sense they ought to bear; nor is it the first-flush literalism of the prophet or preacher who seizes the nearest words to convey his message with, and has not yet thought if he will stand committed to all that those words would literally imply. The literalism which rejects the theory of analogy as unproven is a deliberate and dogmatic stance, taken up not for its own merits but to avoid the consequences attached to its alternative. As a position, it admits no refutation: for the theory of analogy cannot be absolutely proved (XI. 5, *ante*). Yet this dogmatic literalism carries no conviction either, for it will not stand up to religious reflection. It is adopted (i) by believers who would like to profess a simple faith and have not understood the theory of analogy, (ii) by non-believers who would prefer a simple faith, such as they heard at Sunday School, as an Aunt Sally for their coconuts, and occasionally (iii) by naughty theologians anxious to discredit their opponents' views as too complex to believe.

(B) NONSENSICALISM

2   The second alternative is to abandon religion
because theology does not make sense. And if theology is thought of as logically prior to religious faith
this agnosticism is clearly correct. Thomas, thinking it possible to prove that there is a God, asserted
this logical priority:

> we must set down in the beginning that whereby
> his existence is demonstrated, as the necessary
> foundation of the whole work. For, if we do not
> demonstrate that God exists, all consideration of
> divine things is necessarily suppressed.*

Kant thought the existence of God could not be
proved, in a speculative way. People then began to
say that this starting-point would have to be reached
by 'a leap of faith'. But they thought they could go
on, once that leap was made, to describe God's
actions and his attributes, and they thought of
George's religion as George's response to the divine
nature and action thus described. Theology, on this
view, is still logically prior to religion; and it is
still sensible, if theology is barred for ambiguity,
to give up religion too.

3   The logical positivists drew this conclusion
from their simple creed. They thought every
term univocal, and every genuine statement able
to be verified. So any statement whose sense
cannot be clearly determined should be rejected
as nonsensical. On this view, if the theory of
Analogy is correct, then statements about God
are all nonsense. 'If you can't say it (clearly)
then you had better keep quiet!† One need not
however be a positivist to think theology nonsensical.

(c) FIDEISM

4   The third alternative is to keep religion but discard theology. This will appeal to many who value their faith, but find sermons uninspiring and religious dispute distasteful. Yet such people do have a theology, i.e. a system of beliefs. And they usually practise their faith in a community with others who share those beliefs; a community which they found ready-made, and so could take for granted and enjoy without dispute, but which originally grew up as a distinct entity in the course of religious controversy, and continues as one at least partly by means of theological dispute with other Christians and with non-Christians. If theological argument is ruled out, these Christian bodies may not for long continue in their present form; and after that non-theological Christians may not find a quiet haven in which to practise 'simple faith'.

5   From this some infer that theological dispute is inseparable from religious faith; and even that a religious body needs special officers to continue the dispute – or, as they call it, 'defend the faith'. Another inference is possible. It was taken for granted until very recently that theological system is logically prior to practical religion, and this assumption has naturally been reflected in the structures of the church. A change in that assumption (we could infer) is likely to cause changes in the organisation of Christian fellowships and in their inter-relationships.

6   For the present, we need only say that the proposal to keep religion and discard theology is hardly compatible with present institutions. The proposal usually comes from people who like those institutions as they are and who have not realised their own theology. But there are exceptions. The Society

of Friends perhaps comes nearest at present to religion without theology.

(D) FUNDAMENTALISM

7 The fourth alternative is to continue religion with a theology that is descriptive but non-argumentative. This is the position adopted by strict Biblicists or Fundamentalists, who regard the text of the Scriptures as inspired but distrust inferences from it, and all development of doctrines, as human and therefore fallible.

8 If human reason is *very* fallible then the conflicts and contradictions noticed by so many humans between various Scripture texts may after all be only apparent; and those who can believe this can quite properly continue as Fundamentalists, provided they do not appeal to this (or any other) argument. But they can hardly give reasons to others for becoming Fundamentalists. We shall have to leave them marooned upon their Rock.

9 Fundamentalism is a very simple theory, admirably adapted to the student's simple needs. It says that we have a textbook of religion, that everything in the textbook is right and that nothing written elsewhere on the topic deserves even to be read, much less thought about. Philosophical reflection on other topics can however disguise this basic simplicity. Henry Mansel's *Limits of Religious Thought* provide a good instance of this.

10 It is usual to speak of Mansel's 'agnosticism'. He denied that we can select our own Revelation by seeing which one gives the best picture of Almighty God. For 'to construct a complete Criticism of any Revelation, it is necessary that the Critic should be in possession of a perfect Philosophy of the Infinite';* which for humans can be seen to be

impossible. Unable to pick and choose we must – if the Evidences so persuade us – swallow Christianity whole. If Christ was really what he said he was,

> what but contempt and insult can be found in that half-allegiance which criticises while it bows; which sifts and selects while it submits; which approves or rejects as its reason or its feelings or its nervous sensibilities may dictate; which condescends to acknowledge him as the teacher of a dark age and an ignorant people; bowing the knee before him, half in reverence, half in mockery, and crying, 'Hail, King of the Jews!'*

11   The Christianity we are to swallow whole is not the full and final truth, for that is beyond us:

> There can be no such thing as a positive science of Speculative Theology; for such a science must necessarily be based on an apprehension of the Infinite; and the Infinite, though we are compelled to believe in its existence, cannot be positively apprehended in any mode of the human consciousness.*

What God has told us of himself is regulative: not true absolutely, but near enough to teach us how to live. And for this reason we are not to interpret one passage or one image of Scripture as meaning only what is said in other terms elsewhere. It is mistaken then to say that God's 'anger' means that he punishes the wicked *as if* he were angry:

> It is surely more reasonable, as well as more reverent, to believe that these partial representations of the Divine Consciousness, though, as finite, they are unable speculatively to represent the Absolute Nature of God, have yet each of them a

regulative purpose to fulfil in the training of the mind of man: that there is a religious influence to be imparted to us by the thought of God's Anger, no less than by that of his Punishments . . . that both, inadequate and human as they are, yet dimly indicate some corresponding reality in the Divine Nature: and that to merge one in the other is not to gain a purer representation of God as He is, but only to mutilate that under which He has been pleased to reveal Himself.*

12   Mansel does not say that we should keep the idea of God's anger because we find that thinking about it is good for us religiously, but that it must be religiously good for us to think about it, otherwise God would not have put it in the book. If thinking about it leads to difficulties, they must be good for us too: 'without room for doubt, where would be the righteousness of faith?'* Where indeed? One who thinks belief meritorious in itself may be well advised to be a Fundamentalist.

13   It is not very clear whether Mansel approves of argument within theology. He certainly practises it in what we would call meta-theology. There is room, he says, for progress in Christian Theology

from the better interpretation of Holy Writ, or the refutation of unauthorised inferences therefrom,

provided these developments do not transgress the limits set in Article VI. And he quotes with approval an exposition of that Article with a significant comment:

no doctrine has any claim whatever to be received as obligatory on belief, unless it be either itself some duly authorised principle, or a logical deduction, through whatever number of stages, from some such principle of religion. But in truth, as our own liability to error is extreme, especially when in the holy obscurity ('the *cloud* on the mercy-seat') of such mysteries as these, we have reason to thank God that there appear to be few doctrinal developments of any importance which are not from the first drawn out and delivered on divine authority to our acceptance.*

14   For Mansel, the whole system of Christian thought is one of licensed analogy. God has revealed to us directly what he wants us to believe. He permits us to draw further inferences, being presumably satisfied that the laws of thought he has put in our heads, if not valid absolutely, will at any rate not be misleading in our circumstances. Theology then is a very human science. It is true of our world as we see it. Like Kant's mechanics and geometry it is 'empirically real but transcendentally ideal'.

15   It would however take a transcendent philosopher to see that the world is only empirically real. The same criticism applies to Mansel's scheme; that in order to state it one needs to think and speak outside it. One could not object to God proclaiming it, but in Mansel's mouth it is an elaborate and ultimately incoherent apology for continuing to accept uncritically whatever one has been brought up to regard as authorised.

(E) MYSTICALISM

16   Our fifth alternative – seeing how unsafe it is to argue about God – is to continue religion each with his private theology: exchanging confession and exhortation and combining in praise, but never thinking aloud or getting down to argument.

17   This position seems to fit very neatly with the

doctrine of analogy. For our whole difficulty goes back to that so-called equation with its two unknowns:

$$\frac{\text{Love in God}}{\text{Being of God}} :: \frac{\text{Love in man}}{\text{Being of man}}$$

We don't know *how* God's love is different, and we can't work it out either, for we don't know what being God is like. But, says the mystic, suppose the believer *does* know, at least a little bit. The Christian life is said to be a matter of 'letting God dwell in us' and 'having the mind of Christ'. Anyone who comes to know, in this practical way, what it is like to be God, will by implication be able to work out (practically) what the love of God is like.

18   Such a mystic is saying what no one is in a position to deny. We may indeed readily accept that their religious experience is valuable to them, and that others find it uplifting to hear it spoken of. But what is said will not rescue theology from the toils of analogy. For the supposed 'knowing what being God is like' is private to each one. It is no good the mystic propounding to others an argument containing 'love of God' for, while he knows (it is said) how this love is qualified, the others don't, so they cannot evaluate his argument. If they are to take its validity on trust from him, they had just as well take the conclusion and not bother with the argument.

19   Can the mystics argue with each other? Yes, if mystic A means the same as mystic B by 'love of God'. But how can he tell he does? He has no other words to express it by. They both mean 'love' (as commonly understood) 'but appropriately qualified'. A is supposed to have a working knowledge of what qualification is appropriate; but that working knowledge is unfortunately

inexpressible. B is supposed to have one too. But if both find it inexpressible neither can tell if the other's qualification is in fact the same as his. 'He should take that on trust'. Yes, he may: but then he need not trouble his head with arguments. You can eat what you're given, or look at it first; but it's silly to look at it carefully *in the dark*.

20   The proposal to continue religion 'each with his private theology' really means 'without any theology', an alternative discussed a little earlier. It would tend to make religions theoretically indistinguishable: though their results in the lives of their practitioners might well be different – as they are at present in any (theoretically) one religion with a flourishing theology. Whether religions *ought* to be theoretically distinguishable is another matter, and a practical religious one, rather than philosophical or theoretical.

XIX. Nondescriptivism

FACED with the imbecility of argumentative theology I suggested six alternatives. The first five – Literalism, Nonsensicalism, Fideism, Fundamentalism and Mysticalism – have been rejected as inadequate. I shall now say something to commend the sixth alternative, which for lack of a happier or familiar term we may call Nondescriptivism.

2 I am not suggesting that because the first five are inadequate therefore we must accept the sixth. For one thing, there is no way of knowing that there are only six alternatives. And it could be that all the alternatives open to us are equally unsatisfactory. Moreover, the views I shall propound form only one of many possible versions of the sixth alternative.

3 Instead of arguing by exclusion or desperation I shall try to commend my version of Nondescriptivism as positively accurate and satisfactory: accurate, as an anlysis of what actually goes on when people talk to each other about God; and satisfactory, as 'justifying' philosophically at least some of the things they religiously want to say. For while analysis and interpretation can still be kept distinct they must both come into the discussion at this stage.

4 'Nondescriptive' means much the same as 'nonpropositional'. And many now say that revelation (or, theology) is not propositional. Having agreed what theology *isn't* they then differ widely as to

what it is. What is my positive account?
5   Let me start by distinguishing descriptive assertions from affirmations of intent.* If I say the pillar-
box is red I do indeed affirm; I commit myself to
that being so; I give my word for it. But *what* I give
my word for is nothing personal. The pillar-box is
either red – in fact, out there in the 'real' world we
all share and talk about – or it is not. No amount of
earnestness on my part can make any difference to
that. But in an affirmation of intent – for instance, 'I
will', said before the altar when getting married or
ordained – such an affirmation depends for its present significance on my sincerity, and for its effect-
iveness on what I later do about it. In this context
firmness matters more than facts.
6   Some affirmations are conditional. I promise to
pay, *provided* you supply the goods. Some such conditions may be specifically ruled out – 'for better for
worse, for richer for poorer, in sickness and in
health' – while some limitation still remains – 'till
death us do part'. Could one make an affirmation
with no ifs and buts at all? There is not room for
many such 'ultimate' or unconditional affirmations
in any one man's life. His religion,† I suggest, is in
practice constituted by those that he does make.
7   When we make a descriptive assertion we are not
usually aware of all that it implies; for instance, one
can assert Euclid's axioms while ignorant of many of
his theorems. The implications of a personal undertaking or affirmation may also be hidden from the
affirmer at the time; he has, we say, to work it out,
to find out in practice 'what he let himself in for'.
Both assertors and affirmers may be held to 'understand' what they are saying without at that time
knowing all the implications that they may later realise. But in an 'ultimate' affirmation the extent of

this understanding ignorance is much more obvious, just because all let-outs have been specifically ruled out. Fancy expecting me to forgive the same chap four hundred and eighty-nine times more!

8   An ultimate affirmation may be made without using any officially 'religious' words. It is theoretically possible then (on the definitions given) for a man to have an entirely private religion, expressed entirely in ordinary terms. It is however very uncommon for someone just to sit down and decide, without inspiration, example or encouragement, on a set of moral ideals on which to spend his life. Most of us get the idea from other people first.

9   We may get the idea from what people say, or from what they do, or (most impressively) from their doing what they say. And most of what they do and say in this connection is expressed by them in 'religious' terms. Ultimate affirmations are most often made communally and in the name of God.

10   We can't be being epic all the time. But we do need to renew our vows, to remember to try to keep them and also to realise in practice just what they involve. This again is often done communally, through readings, talks, songs, prayer and rituals. Even when done privately it is very largely done in the God-language of the vow-community to which the *devotee* belongs.

11   It is possible to make conflicting vows. The undertakings of a bigamist conflict permanently and in principle: those of a bankrupt became conflicting in practice when his assets and credit slid below his demanded debts. The conflicts of religion are usually more complex and indirect than these, but in logical outline they are similar. A conflict arises when one man finds that two vows of his cannot, in his circumstances, both be carried out. Practical attempts

to resolve these conflicts are the mainsprings of religious reform; theoretical solutions form the structure of theology.

12   Natural science has been well described as a way of resolving conflicts between present experience and previous theory. The method is to revise the theory; i.e. to seek a new description of how the world is, in that particular respect, consistent both with the new experience and with all the old experiences which the previous theory was intended to enshrine.* This method has been highly successful, and it was only natural that the Greeks, who invented it, should try it in theology as well.

13   Descriptive theology – the elaboration of stories of another world, peopled by beings with superhuman powers who made our world and us and who then, by an almost universal fallacy, demand our consequent obedience – this scheme has had a good long innings now. Unlike the sciences, it has never been truly catholic, i.e. universally acceptable, because there is no agreed way for deciding cases in dispute. One can of course argue deductively, down to further consequences or back to higher principles, but that only takes one around the given theological system. It cannot decide between systems. A runaround ticket on a train will not show if it is better than a bus.

14   The scientist appeals, in the end, to experience, to the observations made by himself and others, and which his reader could (in principle) repeat. The theologian is driven to appeal in the end to revelation or authority: to experiences reported by some but *not* repeatable at will, or to the loyalties imposed on members of a given church. Even if accepted on these terms a system of descriptive theology has certain disadvantages.

15   First, it is subject to analogy. We have to admit that we don't mean what we say and are uncertain what we really mean. This limitation is inherent, for it is derived by the method of descriptive theology (argument) from some of the axioms of that theology. The analogic agnosticism propounded in this book is the conclusion of an epistemic argument of which some premises are (descriptive) theological. For theologians this difficulty is unavoidable. It is fatal to theology as hitherto conceived.

16   The second disadvantage in descriptive theology is that it helps us misunderstand the logical relation of theory and practice in this field. Descriptive theologians present their systems as absolute truths about the universe, objective facts to which our actions and attitudes had better be conformed. This inverts the true logical priority. Religious terms are used first in vows. Their descriptive use (or misuse) comes later, when we try to explain and reconcile our vows.

17   The third and consequent disadvantage is more human and practical. People whose vows appear justified by a would-be-scientific description of the beginning and end and inner nature of the Universe tend to be dogmatic in the proclamation of their vows. They think theirs are right and everyone else's must in consequence be wrong. But the description to which they appeal is pseudo-science, and the justification which, if true, it would provide is fallacious on a purely descriptive plane. Individual religion can 'follow' from cosmic facts only if the individual himself *decides* to be on the right side or desires to be on the side of the Right.

18   'But it can't be wrong for me to think I am right in my belief, for I would not even hold it otherwise'. True. But need you add 'everyone else

must in consequence be wrong'? 'Well, they must be, if the beliefs are different and the other one is right'. This holds for assertions. In that objective field, if we do not admit the law of (no-) contradiction we might as well abandon thought. But this law does not so directly apply to affirmations, because of their personal character. Bill's determination to be celibate does not *contradict* the marriage-vows of George.

19 People do however take some of each other's vows as a challenge to 'go away and do the same'.* And those who vow often feel they are doing 'what is right' or 'what is required of them', and infer that anyone else in their place *ought* to vow the same. Can one say this without implying that one who, in such a position, does not vow, is somehow *wrong*?

20 The gospel of John retails a pleasant little drama about a man born blind, whom Jesus cured. The theologians tried to talk him out of it. *Hen oida*, says the man, 'one thing I know; once I was blind, now I can see'.† On this, he is the only good authority. Religious affirmations, I suggest, are to be made in this *henoidal* mood. The affirmer knows he has something to affirm. With all the conviction he commands he commits himself to it. On this, he is not open to correction by anyone. Exactly what it will involve from him he does not know, but will spend his life in finding out. Whether it conflicts, i.e. would interfere, if adopted, with the affirmations or the life-style of others, is not for him to say. He must leave that to them to decide. Taken henoidally, a religious conviction leads not to dogmatism but to humility.

21 The conflicts to which religious affirmations may lead are practical in character, for they arise out of what the affirmer feels obliged by his vows to

do. One could hardly vow to think in a certain way. (One might promise to profess certain opinions, but if one did not still hold them – freely, not owing to the vow – such profession would either not count as *thought* or else would be intellectual dishonesty. That is why it is ludicrous to regard belief – religious or other – as meritorious).

22   The practical conflicts to which affirmations may give rise are also personal in character. By this I mean that only the affirmer can resolve them, by re-interpreting, revising or dropping some of the affirmations which conflict. Most ultimate affirmers tend to put their convictions in epic, lifelong, terms, and they don't like to think later on that they are revising them, so they call it 're-interpretation', 'deeper insight', and 'legitimate development'. The uncommited spectator may have a clearer view of this little game, and might say that, for intance, a religion which acknowledged hell and permitted slavery was substantially different, even if historically continuous, with one that had abolished both.

23   How does the affirmer resolve the personal and practical conflicts to which his affirmations have given rise? Initially he may refer to some descriptive scheme or appeal to his regular authority: but in the end he may find he has revised that scheme or re-defined the scope of that authority. The final court must be his own 'conscience'. Does the vow he took, with the implications now realised, still command his fealty? Or was that not what he was *really* committed to?

24   Some affirmers are constantly renewing (and revising) vows by looking out for challenges. One means to this is the 'devotional' reading of items of literature regarded as sacred or authoritative. With

the pre-selection of 'inspiring' passages and the
'spiritual' interpretation supplied by a devotional
tradition, a reader anxious for guarantees and not
addicted to historical questioning can find food for
his soul in this way in quite unlikely-looking books.†
Others find too much to doubt in the moral and
scientific outlook of the sacred books to notice the
religious challenge that they still present. For such
readers, the retreat from a theory of verbal inspiration to one of 'inspired' description of God's acts
may not be enough. Their problem is, can we properly speak in this way of God's 'acting' in this
world?

25 John Baptist's disciples were sent to ask Jesus
'Are you the one that's coming, or is it someone else
that we are looking forward to?'.* This question
meant a lot to them, for they were expecting God to
send them an anointed king and saviour any day.
We don't have this expectation, nor can we get it by
reading the Old Testament. So we cannot directly
confront the challenge that they faced; certainly not
by having the official answer ready pat. But we can
try to reconstruct John's world of beliefs and see
how the challenge came to him. It is not our challenge; but his response may challenge us.

26 Many Jews of his day thought this world
would shortly end; and some early Christians
expected this to be brought about by the trium-
phant second coming of their Lord. They were dis-
appointed. Were they mistaken? That can only
mean, Had they good reasons, by their (to us) out-
landish standards, for holding this belief? Or had
they misinterpreted the message they received? The
evidence now available to us does not permit a decision on this point. It would indeed be remarkable if
we now could reach unanimity on a historical and

interpretative question which puzzled and divided them. Fortunately we are not required to decide this point. What concerns us is, granted their beliefs, how did they respond?

27   Most religious people look only within their own tradition for challenges; partly because of loyalty, but very largely because of difficulty. If they read the sacred texts of another religion, they take them literally, not having been brought up to the selective re-interpretation by which those texts can speak to people of another age. It is doubtful if study alone can overcome this barrier. One needs to live alongside a practising member of that faith to appreciate non-attachment, or submission, as practical ideals: as making a difference to everyday life, admirable in result and possible to adopt, and so as presenting a challenge to oneself.

28   A religion, I suggest, provides a language for making ultimate commitments in. Reflection on those we have made and might make, the comparing and reconciling of vows made 'before God', may be called theology. Such a theology makes no claim to be a science, human or divine. It neither describes another world nor re-describes the one in which we live. It is nondescript. So it is not subject to analogy.

xx. Proper Faith

IT WILL be said that this scheme replaces belief in God by belief in me; that it is arrogant to think my personal resolutions of cosmic significance, and dishonest to use religious terms for saying so: that what I am propounding is humanism rather than religious faith.

2 I say that this scheme re-states the relation of personal faith, or religion, to public theorising, or theology. What I wish to deny is that beliefs about God are *primary*.

3 It would be very awkward if they were. For, firstly, they are dubious. There are arguments for them of course, and arguments against, but there is no higher court of rational appeal to decide which set of arguments is best. We have to swallow them like pills, hoping someone has put the right label on the box.

4 The second difficulty is more awkward still. All statements about God, it seems, are subject to analogy. We have to use symbols to allude to them, and what we say in the symbols cannot be properly expressed in ordinary prose. No arguments to or from these symbols, then, can be known to be reliable. So how can we decide which set of symbols to prefer?

5 Some say, prefer those which God has given. Revealed symbols are reliable.* This is a pleasantry; for how are we to tell which ones they are?

The statement that God gave them is itself symbolic, and so subject to analogy. What these people mean in practice is, accept those symbols which your religious community regards as satisfactory; e.g. those that the better parts of the Bible use quite frequently, or those that Holy Mother Church has always lately loved to teach.

6   This makes it a matter of personal decision once again: for one will only rest in a religious community whose set of 'satisfactory symbols' does meet one's own religious needs. The appeal to authority reduces in the end to a rule for membership.

7   Let us then ask, How *do* people come to prefer one set of symbols as religiously satisfactory to them? What is it about a particular language of devotion that makes one want to speak 'to God' in it?

8   Let us ask, for a start, why the symbols we use are so largely human or personal.

> Fish (fly-replete, in depth of June,
> Dawdling away their wat'ry noon)
> Ponder deep wisdom, dark or clear,
> Each secret fishy hope or fear.
> Fish say, they have their Stream or Pond;
> But is there anything Beyond?
> This life cannot be All, they swear,
> For how unpleasant, if it were!
> One may not doubt that, somehow, Good
> Shall come of Water and of Mud;
> And, sure, the reverent eye must see
> A Purpose in Liquidity.
> We darkly know, by Faith we cry,
> The future is not Wholly Dry.
> Mud unto mud! – Death eddies near –
> Not here the appointed End, not here!

But somewhere, beyond Space and Time,
Is wetter water, slimier slime!
And there (they trust) there swimmeth One
Who swam 'ere rivers were begun,
Immense, of fishy form and mind,
Squamous, omnipotent, and kind;
And under that Almighty Fin,
The littlest fish may enter in . . .*

9 As a critique of human descriptions of God that admits of no reply. However we may wrap up the point, we *have* to think of our God as like a man†. There are, however, men and men. Which human qualities are we going to revere? The answer will vary with the individual and his morality. What does he think is good, fine, heroic, perfect or ideal? Only one whose life displays these qualities will bring him to his knees.

10 Christians, on this view, worship Jesus because of what they see in him. Responding to the moral challenge he presents, they are ready to take his theology more or less on trust: to call God Daddy if he thinks we can.

Appendix:
Texts from Aquinas's
discussions of analogy

Digest (of arguments) against the Gentiles, I.
32
It follows, however, that no term can be used of God
in quite the same sense (*univoce*) as it is used of other
things.

For a description based on a cause cannot be
applied in the same sense to its effect, which is dissimilar; thus the heat generated by the sun is not
called 'hot' in the same sense as the sun itself. Now
the things God has made are not comparable to
him, for what he possesses whole and undivided
they share out in bits between them. No term then
can be applied in quite the same sense to God as it
is to other things.

Even where an effect does resemble its cause it is
still not described by the same term in quite the
same sense, unless the effect belongs to the same
order of being as its cause. Thus a house in plan is
not called 'house' in quite the same sense as an
actual built house, for they have different ways of
being a house. Now even if other things resembled
God exactly they would still not bear this resemblance in the same order of being, for in God (unlike
other things) there is just the actual divine being,
and nothing else. No term, then, can possibly be

applied in the same sense both to God and to other things.

Further, any description applied in the same sense to several different things is either a genus or a species or a difference (defining peculiarity) or an accident or a proprium (non-defining quality found throughout a species). But no description applies to God as a genus or as a difference; nor consequently as a definition either, for that is made up of genus and difference; nor can anything belong to him accidentally. So no term can be applied to God either as accident or as proprium, for a proprium counts as an accident. The only conclusion is that no description applies to God in the same sense as to other things.

Again, any term applied in the same sense to several things is simpler, to think of, anyway, than any one of them. But nothing can be simpler than God either in definition or in our idea of it. So no description can be applied in the same sense to God as to other things.

Further, any term applied in the same sense to several things belongs to each of them by way of sharing; for the species is held to 'share in' the genus, and the individual in its species. But no term can be applied to God by way of sharing, for a property shared is shared in a partial manner, according to the capacity of the sharer, and not in the full measure of its perfection. No description, then, should be applied in the same sense to God and to other things.

Moreover, a description applied to several things by way of logical priority and consequence is certainly not applied in quite the same sense, for what

is prior is included in the definition of its consequent, e.g. *substance* in the definition of *quality*, where
quality is taken as an entity. Now if *substance* and *quality* were both called *entities* in the same sense, the
definition of *entity* as applied to *substance* would itself
contain the term *substance*, which obviously won't do.
Now no descriptions apply both to God and to other
things in the same order of existence, but only by
way of priority and consequence, descriptions
applied to God being all meant essentially, for it is
as Being itself that he is said to be, as very Goodness
that we call him good. But to everything else terms
are applied by way of sharing: thus Socrates is not
called *man* because he is Humanity, but as sharing
in humanity. It is impossible then for any description to be applied in quite the same sense to God as
to other things.

33
From what was said earlier, however, it also follows
that a description applied to God as well as to other
things is not totally ambiguous (*secundum puram
aequivocationem*) – as happens when two things just
happen to bear the same name. In such cases no one
expects to find the two things related, for it was
mere accident that led to the same term being
applied to the two things, so that its application to
the one in no way implies a connection with the
other. This however is not the case with terms which
apply to God as well as to created things. In this
case, when we use the same term for both, we have
in mind the relation of cause and effect. A descriptive term applied to God as well as to other things is
not then totally ambiguous.

Moreover, in a case of complete ambiguity there

is no real similarity between the things described; the only link is in the name. But things do resemble God up to a point, so it cannot be in complete ambiguity that terms describing them are applied to God as well.

Again, if a term is applied to several things quite ambiguously, knowledge of one of these things will tell us nothing about the others, for knowledge depends on how the things are to be defined, not simply on what words we use for them. Now we do in fact move from features of other things to knowledge of divine matters. So it is not in complete ambiguity that features of this sort are attributed to God as well as to other things.

Moreover punning hampers reasoning. If no description could be applied to God as well as to created things without complete ambiguity, it would be impossible to argue from created things to God; whereas all theological discussions show the contrary.

Further, it would be pointless to describe a thing if the description told us nothing about it. But a description applied in complete ambiguity to God and to created things could not tell us anything about God, for the meanings of those terms are known to us only by their application to created things. So it would be pointless to say or prove that God is a good being, etc. etc.

It may be said that terms like this tell us only what God is not, e.g. that he is called 'living' because he does not belong to the class of inanimate objects, and so on: but in that case the term 'living', applied to God as well as to created things, would have to indicate a denial of lifelessness in both cases;

so it would not be completely ambiguous.

34

The remaining possibility is that terms applied to God as well as to other things are used neither in a completely different sense (*aequivoce*) nor yet in quite the same sense (*univoce*) but in a related sense (*analogice*), i.e. by relation or reference to some one thing.

This can happen in two ways:

A Many refer to one; e.g. there is only one health, by reference to which a living being is called healthy, as having health, medicine is called healthy as giving health, food as preserving it, and urine as indicating it.

B There are two things, but the relation or reference is not to something else again, but to one of them; e.g. *substance* and *quality* are both said to be entities, but this is said of *quality* by relation to *substance*, and not because both *substance* and *quality* are related to some third thing.

Now when terms like this are applied both to God and to other things in related senses (*analogice*) this happens as in way B; for way A would involve making something else prior to God.

When a description is used like this in a related sense (*in analogica praedicatione*), priority in terminology may diverge from factual priority. For terminological order follows the sequence in which we get to know the things, a term being a sign of an idea that is understood. Now where what is first in fact is also known first, we find that the same thing comes first both in the definition (*secundum nominis rationem*) and in the nature of the thing: thus *substance* comes before *quality* both in fact, being its cause, and also in our knowledge, as *substance* forms part of the definition of *quality*. That is why it is more proper to call *substance* than *quality* an entity, whether we are working from facts or from definitions. But sometimes it happens that what comes first in fact is not known to us first. When this occurs in terms used in a related sense there will be a difference between the real order and the terminological; thus the healing power found in curative drugs is prior in fact to the health of the patient, being its cause, yet this power being known to us from its effect gets its name ('health-giving') from that effect. That is why, although the curative drug is factually first, terminologically it is the living body that is most properly called 'healthy', and the drug is called 'health-giving' or curative only by derivation. In the same way, as we move from knowledge of other things to knowledge of God, the facts referred to by the terms which are applied both to God and to other things exist in God first (in an appropriate manner, naturally), yet it is only in a derivative and secondary way that the terms referring to those facts are applied to God. That is why we say that he is described in terms of his effects.

35

It follows that terms applied to God are not all synonymous, even though they all indicate the same reality, for the ideas they give us of him are not all the same. For just as things, though very various, yet in their various ways all resemble that one simple thing, God, so also our mind in forming various ideas comes to resemble him to some extent, being led on towards knowledge of him by these various ideas of the perfections of created things. So it is not wrong or silly of us to conceive that one thing in

many ways, for the simple divine being is one that
can, in various ways, be made the subject of many
comparisons; and following these various lines of
thought we construct various descriptive terms for
God. As these do not all apply to him for the same
reason, they are not all synonymous, though they do
indicate a reality entirely single and unique. For the
terms involved do not all mean the same, indicating
as they do ideas in our minds primarily, and only by
means of these referring to the object being thought
about.

(From the Latin of S. *Thomae Aquinatis Summa Philo-
sophica seu De Veritate Catholicae Fidei Contra Gentiles*, I.
I am grateful to Fr Cornelius Ernst, O.P., for help in
connection with this rendering.)

Further points made in the Summa Theologiae
Ia.13.2

REPLY: It is clear that the problem does not arise for
negative terms or for words which express the relationship of God to creatures; these obviously do not
express what he is but rather what he is not or how
he is related to something else – or, better, how
something else is related to him. The question is
concerned with words like 'good' and 'wise' which
are neither negative or relational terms, and about
these there are several opinions.

Some have said that sentences like 'God is good',
although they sound like affirmations are in fact
used to deny something of God rather than to assert
anything. Thus for example when we say that God
is living we mean that God is not like an inanimate
thing, and likewise for all such propositions. This
was the view of the Rabbi Moses.

Others said that such sentences were used to signify the relation of God to creatures, so that when

we say 'God is good' we mean that God is the cause of goodness in things, and likewise in other such propositions.

Neither of these views seem plausible, and for three reasons. Firstly, on neither view can there be any reason why we should use some words about God rather than others. God is just as much the cause of bodies as he is of goodness in things; so if 'God is good' means no more than that God is the cause of goodness in things, why not say 'God is a body' on the grounds that he is the cause of bodies? So also we could say 'God is a body' because we want to deny that he is merely potential being like primary matter.

Secondly it would follow that everything we said of God would be true only in a secondary sense, as when we say that a diet is 'healthy', meaning merely that it causes health in the one who takes it, while it is the living body which is said to be healthy in a primary sense.

Thirdly, this is not what people want to say when they talk about God. When a man speaks of the 'living God' he does not simply want to say that God is the cause of our life, or that he differs from a lifeless body.

So we must find some other solution to the problem. We shall suggest that such words do say what God is; they are predicated of him in the category of substance, but fail to represent adequately what he is. The reason for this is that we speak of God as we know him, and since we know him from creatures we can only speak of him as they represent him. Any creature, in so far as it possesses any perfection, represents God and is like to him, for he, being simply and universally perfect, has pre-existing in himself the perfections of all his creatures, as noted above. But a creature is not like to God as it is like to another member of its species or genus, but resembles him as an effect may in some way resemble a transcendent cause although failing to reproduce perfectly the form of the cause – as in a certain way the forms of inferior bodies imitate the power of the sun. This was explained earlier when we were dealing with the perfection of God. Thus words like 'good' and 'wise' when used of God do signify something that God really is, but they signify it imperfectly because creatures represent God imperfectly.

'God is good' therefore does not mean the same as 'God is the cause of goodness' or 'God is not evil'; it means that what we call 'goodness' in creatures pre-exists in God in a higher way. Thus God is not good because he causes goodness, but rather goodness flows from him because he is good. As Augustine says, *Because he is good, we exist.* . . .

Ia 13.3

REPLY: As we have said, God is known from the perfections that flow from him and are to be found in creatures yet which exist in him in a transcendent way. We understand such perfections, however, as we find them in creatures, and as we understand them so we use words to speak of them. We have to consider two things, therefore, in the words we use to attribute perfections to God, firstly the perfections themselves that are signified – goodness, life and the like – and secondly the way in which they are signified. So far as the perfections signified are concerned the words are used literally of God, and in fact more appropriately than they are used of creatures, for these perfections belong primarily to God and only secondarily to others. But so far as the way of signifying these perfections is concerned the

words are used inappropriately, for they have a way
of signifying that is appropriate to creatures. . . .

Ia.13.6

REPLY: Whenever a word is used analogically of
many things, it is used of them because of some
order or relation they have to some central thing. In
order to explain an extended or analogical use of a
word it is necessary to mention this central thing.
Thus you cannot explain what you mean by a
'healthy' diet without mentioning the health of the
man of which it is the cause; similarly you must
understand 'healthy' as applied to a man before you
can understand what is meant by a 'healthy com-
plexion' which is the symptom of that health. The
primary application of the word is to the central
thing that has to be understood first; other applica-
tions will be more or less secondary in so far as they
approximate to this use.

Thus all words used metaphorically of God apply
primarily to creatures and secondarily to God.
When used of God they signify merely a certain
parallelism between God and the creature. When
we speak metaphorically of a meadow as 'smiling'
we only mean that it shows at its best when it flowers, just as a man shows at his best when he
smiles: there is a parallel between them. In the same
way, if we speak of God as a 'lion' we only mean
that, like a lion, he is mighty in his deeds. It is
obvious that the meaning of such a word as applied
to God depends on and is secondary to the meaning
it has when used of creatures.

This would be the case for non-metaphorical
words too if they were simply used, as some have
supposed, to express God's causality. If, for example, 'God is good' meant the same as 'God is the

cause of goodness in creatures' the word 'good' as applied to God would have contained within its meaning the goodness of the creature; and hence 'good' would apply primarily to creatures and secondarily to God.

But we have already shown that words of this sort do not only say how God is a cause, they also say what he is. When we say he is good or wise we do not simply mean that he causes wisdom or goodness, but that he possesses these perfections transcendently. We conclude, therefore, that from the point of view of what the word means it is used primarily of God and derivatively of creatures, for what the word means – the perfection it signifies – flows from God to the creature. But from the point of view of our use of the word we apply it first to creatures because we know them first. That, as we have mentioned already, is why it has a way of signifying that is appropriate to creatures.

(From *St Thomas Aquinas Summa Theologiae* volume 3 *Knowing and Naming God*, edited and translated by Herbert McCabe, O.P. (1964), 53f. I am obliged to Fr. McCabe, and to Eyre & Spottiswoode (Publishers) Ltd for permission to cite these passages.)

The familiar equation

$$\frac{\text{'x' in God}}{\text{nature of God}} \ :: \ \frac{\text{x in man}}{\text{human nature}}$$

is suggested in the following passages:
On Truth, xxvii.7 Although no ratio can be found between finite and infinite, similarity of ratios is possible; for one infinite stands to another equal infinite in the same way as one finite quantity to another; and this is the form of comparison between a created

thing and God, that he stands to what is his in the same way as a created thing stands to what belongs to it.

On the Fourth Book of Sentences, xlix.2.1 God's knowledge is related to his nature in the same way as our knowledge is related to created beings.

(Cited in M. T-L. Penido *Le Rôle de l'Analogie en Théologie Dogmatique* (1931), 144.)

Notes

These notes are keyed to the text by chapter (numbered in roman) and paragraph (arabic). For some books two dates are given, that of first publication and of the edition cited.

i 7 Cf. E. A. Abbott, *Flatland, A Romance of Many Dimensions . . .By a Square* (1884).

ii 1 T. L. Peacock, *Gryll Grange* (1861; Penguin, 1947) 11.
5 Cf. I. T. Ramsey's 'qualifiers', *Religious Language* (1957) 62f.
16 Cf. J. L. Evans, 'Meaning and Use', *Philosophy and Phenomenological Research* (1961/2) 256f, words have their meanings, but only sentences can be 'meaningful' or 'meaningless'.

iii 2 The main texts from Aquinas are given on p. 165 – 76, *ante*. Recent expositions of the theory include
F. Ferré, *Language Logic and God* (1962) vi
A. M. Farrer, *Finite* and Infinite (1943) 88f
F. C. Copleston, *Aquinas* (1955) 128f
E. L. Mascall, *Existence and Analogy* (1949) v
J. F. Ross, 'Analogy as a rule of meaning for religious language', *International Philosophical Quarterly* (1961) 468f, and in A. Kenny (ed.), *Aquinas* (1970) 93f.
J. M. Bochenski, *The Logic of Religion* (1965) 114f, 156f.
R. M. McInerny, *The Logic of Analogy* (1961)
M. T-L. Penido, *Le Rôle de l'Analogie en Théologie Dogmatique* (1931).
See also I. M. Crombie, 'The Possibility of Theological Statements', *Faith and Logic* (ed. B. Mitchell, 1967) 31f; M. Durrant, 'God and Analogy', *Sophia* (October 1969) 11f.
8 Cf. R. G. Collingwood *Speculum Mentis* (1924) 130: *The Principles of Art* (1938) xi.
16 J. H. Scrine *Creed and the Creeds* (1911) 155f.

iv 6 *Isaiah* lv 8f
12 E. Hoskyns and N. Davey, *The Riddle of the New Testament* (1931) i, infer that there must have been something quite remarkable

– a Christ, not just a church – to cause such a rapid change. The study of living languages debilitates this inference.

16 L. Carroll, *Alice through the Looking Glass* (1872) vi.

17 R. Robinson, *Definition* (1954) iv.

v 14 E. M. Forster, *Howards End* (1910) xxiii.

17 Aristotle, *Nicomachean Ethics,* ii 6.

vi 2 Elijah's remarks on Carmel (I Kings xviii 27) are sarcastic rather than systematic. He was not complaining that the other prophets said their God was busy, or spending a penny, or asleep (they didn't), but taunting them because their mumbo-jumbo had not worked.

6 *Acts* xvii 34.

C. E. Rolt, *Dionysius the Areopagite On the Divine Names and Mystical Theology* (1920), ii, iv, v, cited from N. Smart, 'Pseudo-Dionysius on the Negative Way' in *Historical Selections in the Philosophy of Religion* (1962) iii.

7 Thomas Aquinas, *Summa Contra Gentiles* I xiv; tr. A. C. Pegis, *On the Truth of the Catholic Faith* (1955) I 97.

11 The question expects the answer 'I don't know', enabling the retort 'I won't give you my letters to post'.

14 Thomas Aquinas, op. cit. I xiv 3.

15 I. Kant, *Critique of Pure Reason* (1781; 1787) 59, and preface p. xxvi.

16 I. T. Ramsey, *Religious Language* (1957) 19f; *Models and Mystery* (1964) 52f; *Christian Discourse* (1965) 5f. The disclosures (or visions of the world as God's) lead to worship, not theology, so perhaps they can be purely personal.

17 R. Otto, *The Idea of the Holy* (1917; Penguin 1959) 39f. The Wholly Other can be described only by our reactions to its presence. Otto thinks these will be appropriate, and show there must be Something There.

vii 1 E. Bevan, *Symbolism and Belief* (1938; Fontana 1962) 227f. See also T. H. McPherson, *The Philosophy of Religion* (1965) 182f.

6 *Ephesians* iii 15.

9 *I Samuel* xv.

12 Thomas Aquinas, *Summa Contra Gentiles* I v 5 'even the most imperfect knowledge on the sublimest matters confers maximum perfection on the soul'.

viii 4 If Thomas held this view he did not stick to it in planning out his works, for the *Contra Gentiles* does not deal with God's infinity until after the exposition of analogy, while the *Summa Theologiae* treats his goodness and perfection first. A vague or 'non-quidditative' knowledge is no solution either, for it would either be too vague to prove the theory, or not vague enough to come under it; cf. V. White, *God the Unknown* (1956) 16f.

9   I. Kant, *Critique of Pure Reason* (1781;1787) 42f,59f.

IX 5   *Deuteronomy* iv 34. The example is traditional. cf. P. Browne, *The Procedure Extent and Limits of Human Understanding* (1728), 145: 'when God is said to have a *mighty arm*, it means something as real and true, as when it is said God is *powerful*: and yet there can be nothing correspondent and answerable to a great arm of flesh, in God. Whereas when God is said to be powerful, and wise, and good, we don't only mean something true, and solid, and real; but also inconceivable perfections in his real nature correspondent and answerable to power, and wisdom, and goodness in us.' For Browne the whole Socinian system depends 'upon resolving all revelation and the mysteries of Christianity into mere metaphor and allusion only' (143); hence the importance of the theory of analogy.

X 5   D. Hume, *Dialogues concerning Natural Religion* (1779; Fontana 1963), 123: 'Will any man tell me with a serious countenance, that an orderly universe must arise from some thought and art, like the human; because we have experience of it? To ascertain this reasoning, it were requisite, that we had experience of the origin of worlds. .' Cf. *Job* xxxviii f.

19   Cf. L. Hodgson *For Faith and Freedom* (1956) I 155: 'Neither to theologians nor physicists has God thought fit to give the kind of revelation they feel that they would provide if they were God'.

XI 5   L. Wittgenstein, *Tractatus Logico-Philosophicus* (1922), section 6.54.

XII 8   Plato, *The Republic*, tr. Cornford (1941) II 372f, III 414f, IV 434f.

11   Op. cit. II 368

12   Op. cit. IV 441.

17   On analogical thinking (as opposed to talking or arguing) see D. Emmett, *The Nature of Metaphysical Thinking* (1945) i, v, ix, x.

21   Cf. W. K. Clifford 'The Ethics of Belief', *Contemporary Review* (1876) and in *Lectures and Essays* (1879): 'It is wrong everywhere and for everyone, to believe anything on insufficient evidence' (cited from J. Passmore, *A Hundred Years of Philosophy* (1957; Penguin 1968) 95).

22   Cashing a metaphor is a lively metaphor from W. James, *Pragmatism* (1907) 74.

XIII 6   R. Latta and A. MacBeath, *The Elements of Logic* (1929) 376.
        C. L. Hamblin, *Fallacies* (1970) 44, citing S. H. Mellone,

Introductory Textbook of Logic (1902; 1914) 166. Hamblin would like to distinguish Four Terms from Ambiguity or Equivocation, but cannot cite any non-ambiguous fallacy of Four Terms.

9   R. Descartes, *Meditations* (1641; Penguin 1960, tr. Wollaston) 135.

11   Cf. C. L. Hamblin, *Elementary Formal Logic* (1967), 18.

14   D. Hume, *Enquiry concerning the Human Understanding* (1748; 1962) lv, lvii.

16   M. Maimonides, *The Guide of the Perplexed* (1190; Chicago, 1963, tr. Pines) 146.

17   M. T-L. Penido, *Le . Rôle de l'Analogie*, etc, 8. Cf. I. M. Bochenski 'On Analogy' in *Logico-Philosophical Studies*, ed. A. Menne (1962) 97f, who formulates a symbolisation of the theory of analogy and notes the 'serious gnoseological difficulties' it raises for argumentative theology. He rejects Cajetan's solution – that any theological syllogism be re-formulated with a new middle term defined to mean alternately what the old one meant when used (*a*) of men and (*b*) of God. To this Bochenski objects that we don't know meaning (*b*). One could add that if this dodge really rescued the syllogism, ambiguity would never be a fatal fallacy, for one could always construct a new term to mean alternatively (say) page (of a book) and page (-boy). Bochenski's own solution is to claim that relational terms when applied to God can at least be known to retain the formal or logical properties they possess in ordinary use, and that these properties form a sufficient basis for theological reasoning. These claims may be assessed by considering 'love' in God, which may be known at least to mean some dynamic non-symmetrical two-term relation – e.g., 'hate'! To this cure some may prefer the disease.

18   V. White, *God the Unknown* (1956) ii, citing Thomas Aquinas, *Summa Theologiae*, I i 7 and *In Boethii De Trinitate* I 7.

19   *Summa Theologiae* I xiii 10, I xii 13, cited by White, op. cit., 22.

22   J. Pieper, *The Silence of St. Thomas* (tr. D. O'Connor, 1957) 45f.

23   G. Berkeley, *Alciphron, or the Minute Philosopher* (1732) IV xviii. Berkeley replies that intellectual activities, which do not, like passions and actions, require a body, imply no defect. 'Knowledge, therefore, in the proper formal meaning of the word, may be attributed to God proportionably' (xxi). So the same arguments that prove a first cause also prove an intelligent cause: 'intelligent, I say, in the proper sense; wise and good in the true and formal acceptation of the words. Otherwise, it is evident that every syllogism brought to prove those attributes, or (which is the same thing) to prove the being of a God, will be found to consist of four terms, and consequently can conclude nothing.' (xxii). Analogy, he thinks, avoids this disastrous consequence by the fact that mathematicians mean something precise by it (xx). Peter Browne met the same objection by re-stating the traditional distinction between metaphor and analogy: 'In divine metaphor

the resemblance, or proportion, or correspondency is imaginary; 'tis pure invention and mere allusion alone, and no way founded in the real nature of the things compared. But in divine analogy the resemblance, or at least the correspondency and proportion is real, and built on the very nature of things on both sides of the comparison. There is something really correspondent and answerable and proportionable in heavenly and spiritual beings, to those conceptions which are justly substituted to represent them. As, for instance, there is certainly some inconceivable perfection in God answerable to human knowledge; . . . what knowledge and goodness are in the nature of man, that some inconceivable but correspondent perfections are in the nature of God.' *The Procedure, Extent and Limits of Human Understanding* (1728) 137f. As the comparison is not observable we have to argue for it, i.e. show that there must be a real 'analogy' between divine and human nature. This argument occupies most of Browne's *Things Divine and Supernatural conceived by Analogy with things Natural and Human* (1733).

24   J. F. Bethune-Baker, *An Introduction to the Early History of Christian Doctrine* (1903) 160; cf. I. T. Ramsey, *Religious Language* (1957)164.

xiv 1   D. Z. Phillips, *The Concept of Prayer* (1965) 7.

2   L. Wittgenstein, *Tractatus*, section 4.11. What contrast could 'clearly' have come to mark, if language *were* like that?

4   P. G. Winch, *The Idea of a Social Science and its relation to Philosophy* (1968) 100f, criticising V. Pareto *The Mind and Society* (1935) 150; cf. D. Z. Phillips op.cit., 10f., and 'Religious Belief and Philosophical Enquiry', *Theology* (1968), 114f.

P. G. Winch, 'Understanding a Primitive Society', *American Philosophical Quarterly* (1964), and in D. Z. Phillips (ed.,) *Religion and Understanding* (1967) 20f.

12   L. Wittgenstein, *Remarks on the Foundations of Mathematics* (1967) 133; cf. R. Rhees, 'Wittgenstein's Builders', *Proceedings of the Aristotelian Society* (1959-60), 171f.

21   P. Van Buren, *The Secular Meaning of the Gospel based on an Analysis of its Language* (1963) 134.

22   B. Russell, *A History of Western Philosophy* (1946) 859.

23   Cf. H. Palmer, 'To Reduce and to Locate', *Listener* (1966) 605f, 647f.

25   F. M. Oldham, *The Complete School Chemistry* (1907), 152; several other definitions have been tried.

Great Britain Driving Licence (1972), 5

xv 4   L. Wittgenstein, *Philosophical Investigations* (1953) 31f; *The Blue and Brown Books* (1969) 17. See also H. Khatchadourian, 'Common Names and Family Resemblances', *Philosophy and Phenomenological Research* (1957/8) 341f; R. Bambrough, 'Universals and Family Resemblances', *Proceedings of the Aristotelian Society* (1960/1) 207f; K.

Campbell 'Family Resemblance Predicates', *American Philosophical Quarterly* (1965), 238f; M. Mandelbaum, 'Family Resemblances and Generalisation concerning the Arts', *American Philosophical Quarterly* (1965) 219f; A. R. Manser, 'Games and Family Resemblances', *Philosophy* (1967) 210f; M. A. Simon, 'When is a Resemblance a Family Resemblance?', *Mind* (1969), 408f.

11   G. Ryle, 'Thinking and Language', *Proceedings of the Aristotelian Society* (Supp. 1951) 65f; cf. J. O. Urmson, 'Polymorphous Concepts', *Ryle* (ed. Wood and Pitcher, 1970) 249f; M. Mandelbaum, op. cit. 231; R. Robinson *Definition* (1954) 98f.

17   R. Bambrough, 'Aristotle on Justice', *New Essays on Plato and Aristotle* (ed. Bambrough) (1965) 169.

xvi 3   G. Berkeley *A Treatise concerning the Principles of Human Knowledge, wherein the chief causes of Error and Difficulty in the Sciences, with the Grounds of Scepticism, Atheism and Irreligion, are inquired into* (1710), cxliv.

11   A. Flew (ed.) *New Essays in Philosophical Theology* (1955) 96f; H. Palmer 'Affirmation and Assertion', *Philosophy* (1964) 120f.

xvii 2   Leo XIII, *Aeterni Patris* (1879).

4   Thomas Aquinas, *Summa Theologiae*, I xiii 2.
   J. S. Mill, cited in J. Passmore, *A Hundred Years of Philosophy*, 33.

5   Thomas Aquinas, *Summa Theologiae*, tr. H. McCabe (1964) I xiii 5.

6   I. Kant, op.cit., 40.

xviii 2   Thomas Aquinas, *Summa contra Gentiles* (trs. Pegis) I ix 5.

3   L. Wittgenstein, *Tractatus*, section 7: 'On any topic on which speech is impossible silence is mandatory'. Cf. P. Engelmann *Letters from Ludwig Wittgenstein*, tr. B. F. McGuiness (1967), 97: 'The difference (between Wittgenstein and the positivists) is only that they have nothing to be silent about. Positivism holds that what we can speak about is all that matters in life. Whereas Wittgenstein passionately believes that all that really matters in human life is precisely what, in his view, we must be silent about'. But cp. F. P. Ramsey 'What we can't say we can't say, and we can't whistle it either' (cited in J. Passmore, op.cit., 362).

10   H. L. Mansel, *The Limits of Religious Thought* (1858) 233, 252f; cf. D. W. Dockrill, 'The Limits of Thought and Regulative Truths', *Journal of Theological Studies* (1970) 370f; W. R. Matthews, *The Religious Philosophy of Dean Mansel* (1956) 22, concludes that religious doctrines had better be understood by asking what their proponents intended to deny.

11   H. L. Mansel, op. cit., 257, 261.
12   Op. cit., 265.

13   Op. cit., 428f, citing W. A. Butler, *Letters on the Development of Christian Doctrine* (1850) 55f.

xix   5   Cf. H. Palmer, 'Affirmation and Assertion', *Philosophy* (1964) 120f.

6   The term *religion* is said to come from the Latin *religare* = 'bind'. Cf. the hymn much sung at confirmations, 'I bind unto myself today'.

12   W. James *Pragmatism* (1907) 59f., v, vi.

19   *Luke* x. 37, after relating the tale of the Good Samaritan.

20   *John* ix. 25. In 30f. the newly-sighted man himself succumbs to inference.

24   Whether the writer of a certain text meant it literally, is a purely historical question, quite often undecidable. Whether to take it literally now is, for those who hold that text sacred, a separate and religious question. The ages which made literalism a dogma also, and in consequence, saw the flourishing of allegory. Cf. L. Roth, *The Guide for the Perplexed: Moses Maimonides* (1948) 46: 'Perplexity arises in a thoughtful mind when it is bound irrevocably and irretrievably to the words of an ancient text. Allegory and symbolisation preserve the allegiance while releasing the mind.'

25   *Matthew* xi. 3.

xx   5   Cf. A. M. Farrer, *The Glass of Vision* (1948) 44f.

8   R. Brooke, 'Heaven' (1913).

9   Thomas felt this expression improper. 'It is more fitting to say that a creature is like God', *Summa Contra Gentiles* I xxix 5. Perhaps the relation looked more symmetrical this way around.

Index

f   *means*   and on the next page or two
ff   *means*   and on several subsequent pages

Alice   31f
allegory   86f
analysis, philosophical   20, 120f
anthropomorphism   36
Aquinas   *see* Thomas Aquinas
arguing by analogy   17, 88ff
Aristotle   42
Articles, Thirty-nine   108, 148

Berkeley, George   131f
Bethune-Baker, J. F.   106f
Bevan, Edwyn   55f

causal adaequation   57, 72f
creation   56f, 72ff

definition   19, 33, 118, 122, 125ff
Descartes, René   73, 99
differences, negative   50ff
Dionysius (Pseudo-)   48f

fideism   145f
finitude, argument from   26ff, 47, 61ff, 81ff
fundamentalism   146f

henoidal statements   157
humbug   8f
Hume, David   101ff
Humpty Dumpty   31f

Isaiah   27

Kali   74
Kant, Immanuel   53, 63f, 141, 144, 149
knowledge, order of   58f

language-games   113ff, 127
lies, purple   63
literalism   143
Locke, John   95
logical positivists   144

Mansel, Henry   140,146f
marriage   52
metaphor   85f, 95
Mill, John Stuart   140
mode of signification   58f, 76f
Moses ben Maimon (Maimouides)   103, 171
mysticism   34, 149f

Neo-Platonists   47f

nonsensicalism 34, 144

operators 8ff

Plato 88ff
Pythagoras 28, 41

relationships, similarity
of 37f, 87f, 175
Russell, Bertrand 121

simile 86
symbols, irreducible 55ff,
67ff, 121f

terms 15, 33, 98f, 123f, 130

——, borrowed 18, 93f,
131f
——, senses of 9f, 29f, 125ff
theology,
argumentative 139f
——, descriptive 142, 155f
——, natural 104f
——, negative 47ff
Thomas Aquinas 15, 35,
50f, 103f, 141f, 165ff

univocity 9, 28, 33, 36, 125ff

validity, formal 100f
——, occasional 65
——, selective 27
vows 154ff